Lonely ✺ planet

Best
Beaches

100 of the WORLD'S
MOST INCREDIBLE
BEACHES

Contents

Oceania

ABOVE   Camels on Cable Beach/
Walmanyjun, Broome, Australia
RIGHT   Cathedral Cove,
Coromandel Peninsula, New Zealand

Blue Lagoon Beach

FEW TROPICAL ISLANDS have managed to escape the tourism development that typically follows a cameo in a Hollywood film. Not so Nanuya Lailai in Fiji's Yasawa Islands north of Viti Levu, which in 1980 formed the backdrop to scenes from the controversial coming-of-age survival film *The Blue Lagoon* starring a 14-year-old Brooke Shields. Nearly 40 years later, the narrow arc of white sand curving away from Nanuya Island Resort remains blissfully undeveloped, with the tropical jungle on one side, and a calm, blue lagoon on the other.

While Blue Lagoon Beach isn't much different from hundreds of other beautiful beaches set on azure lagoons across Fiji, there's a novelty factor about living out your castaway fantasies here – all by yourself, if you time your visit right. While the coral off the beach isn't Fiji's finest, there are still plenty of tropical fish to spot in the clear lagoon if you feel like putting on a snorkel.

GETTING THERE

The Yasawa Flyer catamaran leaves Nadi's Port Denarau Marina on Viti Levu at 8.45am each morning for the five-hour trip to Nanuya Lailai, including several stops along the way, before returning to Nadi by 6pm. Seaplane transfers are also possible.

Lalomanu Beach

UPOLU

SAMOA

JAGGED BLACK VOLCANIC ROCKS meet the turquoise sea along much of Samoa's coastline, which makes the soft sands of Lalomanu Beach at the southeastern tip of the main island feel all the more special. Devastated by a tsunami that struck Samoa in the early hours of 29 September 2009, Lalomanu's colourful beach *fales* (semi-open-air huts) have since been rebuilt, offering a cheap and characterful sleeping option just steps from the sea, as well as an opportunity to support locals who have rebuilt their lives here, too. With next to nothing to do here but swim and sip local Vailima beer as you gaze across the sparkling Pacific Ocean towards the uninhabited island of Nu'utele, a mile (1.3km) off the coast, it's just about perfect for most visitors. But if you feel like exploring, Tu Sua Ocean Trench, Samoa's most iconic swimming hole formed by a collapsed lava tunnel, is only 8 miles (13km) down the road.

GETTING THERE

Lalomanu Beach is 37.3 miles (60km) or a 90-minute drive from the
capital Apia. Car hire is available at the island's international airport, a
50-minute drive west of Apia, but there are more options in Apia. A bus
runs from Apia's main bus station to Lalomanu Beach, but there is no set
schedule.

Tapuaeta'i/ One Foot Island Beach

AITUTAKI

COOK ISLANDS

〜〜〜

THE TROPICAL ISLANDS OF AITUTAKI curl gently around one of the South Pacific's most sensational lagoons. The aqua water, foaming breakers around the perimeter reef and broad sandy beaches of the atoll's many small deserted islets make for a glorious scene.

The best known of these islets is Tapuaeta'i or One Foot Island. While it somewhat resembles a foot from the air, the small, uninhabited isle's name is thought to have come from a Māori pūrākau (legend), which tells the story of a man and his son who disobeyed a ban on fishing in the lagoon. When the father's boat was spotted by Māori warriors, he snatched up his son and hid him in a coconut tree on the island, leaving just one set of footprints for the warriors to find. When the warriors caught up with him, they killed him and headed back to the main island, convinced they had punished a lone culprit, and the boy was saved.

Today, local tour operators take visitors to the powder-white beach on the island's northwestern tip, where turquoise waters swirl around a scenic sandbank that surfaces at low tide. There isn't a lot of coral inside the lagoon, but snorkellers can expect to spot giant clams and tropical fish that Māori legends have helped to protect for generations.

〜〜〜

GETTING THERE

Aitutaki is reached by a 50-minute flight from Rarotonga, the capital of the Cook Islands. Day trips are possible, but you'll want to spend as much time on Aitutaki as you can.

Ta'ahiamanu Beach

MO'OREA

FRENCH POLYNESIA

AT LAST, A PUBLIC BEACH on Mo'orea! And this narrow stretch of white sand (also known as Moreto Beach) on the volcanic island's gorgeous north coast is an absolute beauty, fringed by swaying coconut palms and affording spectacular views towards the verdant mountains rising across Opunohu Bay. Float in its tropical turquoise waters, or bring your own snorkel and paddle out to the coral-encrusted drop-off (underwater cliff) just off the beach where you can ogle fish, turtles, spotted eagle rays, blacktip reef sharks and other marine critters.

Recently revamped by the local council, the sheltered beach now has shaded areas with picnic tables and a large car park across the road, with toilets, showers and a snack bar. West-facing Ta'ahiamanu Beach is also a stellar place to be in the early evening as the sun sinks behind the string of yachts bobbing in the bay, casting an orange glow on the rippling sea.

GETTING THERE
Ta'ahiamanu Beach is 9.3 miles (15km) or a 20-minute drive from Mo'orea's airport, and 11.8 miles (19km) or a 30-minute drive to the ferry terminal Vai'are (for transfers to Tahiti) on the eastern side of the island. Cars can be rented at both locations.

© CampPhoto / Getty Images

Cathedral Cove

**COROMANDEL PENINSULA,
NORTH ISLAND**

NEW ZEALAND

CREATED BY EXPLOSIVE volcanic eruptions some eight million years ago, dramatic white ignimbrite cliffs frame beautiful Cathedral Cove – actually two coves connected by a gigantic arched cavern that passes through a headland, with magnificent views of Te Hoho Rock rising out of the shallows. With clear turquoise water lapping its golden sands, it's easy to see why Kiwis and visitors alike flock here during the summer months, yet the crowds don't detract from its magic (much).

Only accessible on foot, Cathedral Cove is reached by a scenic, 45-minute clifftop walking track from the Cathedral Cove Lookout

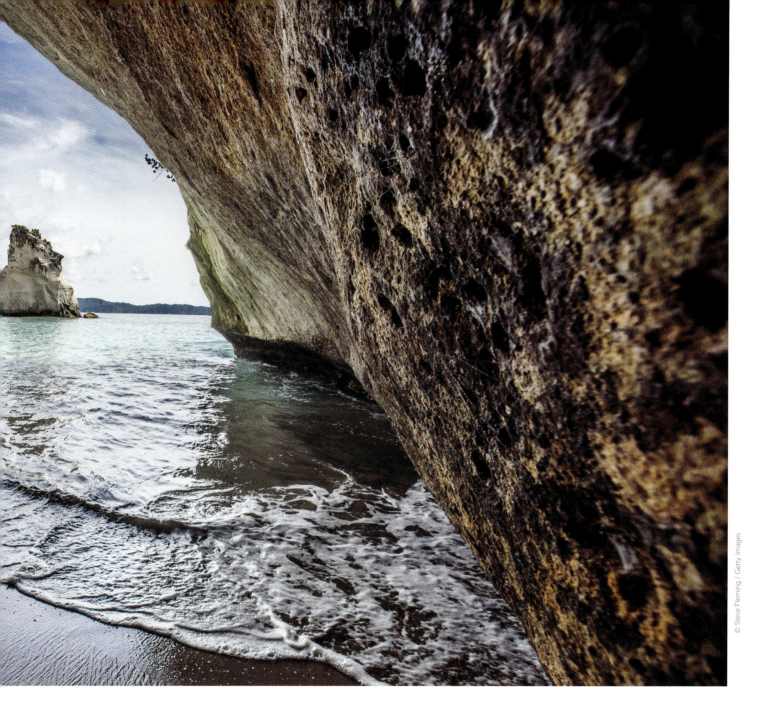

car park. The end of the track descends into the cove, where you can walk through its famous arch. Pack a snorkel and make a detour to Gemstone Bay along the way, which has a snorkelling trail where you can spot anemone gardens, snapper and maybe even a lobster.

Note that from October to April the car park at Cathedral Cove is closed, adding adding an extra 1.2-mile (2km) uphill walk from Hahei village to your journey.

GETTING THERE
If you walk from Hahei Beach directly to Cathedral Cove, it will take about 70 minutes. Another option is the 10-minute Cathedral Cove Water Taxi. If you're driving, leave your car at the Hahei Visitor Car Park on the right-hand side of the entrance to Hahei village and catch a Go Kiwi shuttle (every 20 minutes, 9am–6pm, October to April) to the beginning of the track to Cathedral Cove.

Awaroa Beach

ABEL TASMAN NATIONAL PARK, SOUTH ISLAND
NEW ZEALAND

ALSO KNOWN AS "the people's beach," Awaroa's backstory is legendary. Concerned that public access to its golden sands and turquoise waters could be restricted by a private sale, a pair of Kiwis launched an ambitious crowdfunding campaign in 2016 to buy the remote beach. Raising more than NZ$2 million in just three weeks, the funds – topped up by the New Zealand Government and the Joyce Fisher Charitable Trust – secured the sale, after which Awaroa was ceded to Abel Tasman National Park.

Key to Awaroa's allure is its secluded location on the north coast of the South Island, backed by granite hills and lush coastal forests. Walk the 37.3-mile (60km) Abel Tasman Coast Track over three to five days, explore the sparkling coastline by boat (look out for fur seals dozing on granite outcrops) or take a scenic helicopter ride to experience Awaroa in all of its scenic splendour.

Coast Track walkers will need to cross the tidal estuary at the western end of the beach at low tide when the receding water reveals an azure maze of golden sandbanks. If time permits, pick your way across the pools to the main stretch of beach for a restorative dip before crossing the estuary and continuing your journey. An overnight stay at a beachfront lodge, Department of Conservation hut or campsite allows more time to explore the area. Awaroa is also the only place along the Abel Tasman Coast Track with a restaurant, which adds another incentive to lap up its natural beauty for longer. Listen out for the distinctive call of the kākā, a large parrot native to the area.

GETTING THERE
No cars are allowed in the national park, so visitors need to either walk to Awaroa (22.3 miles/35.9km) from Mārahau, or take a water taxi. Mārahau is an hour's drive from Nelson, which has a domestic airport.

The Pass

BYRON BAY, NEW SOUTH WALES
AUSTRALIA

FOR TENS OF THOUSANDS OF YEARS, the Arakwal Bundjalung people of Gabbanbah (now better known as Byron Bay) in northern New South Wales would gather on the beaches of Walgun (Cape Byron) to fish, feast and share stories. Today the clear warm waters of its most scenic beach, The Pass, fill with surfers chasing one of the world's longest right-hand point breaks, which sweeps northward towards the town. Yet The Pass's rich Aboriginal history remains everywhere, from the region's largest midden (a pile of shell and bones) visible next to the boat ramp, to the culturally significant native wildlife – from koalas to brush turkeys – that can be spotted in the subtropical rainforest fringing its shores.

Even if you're not a beach person, the Aboriginal walking tour hosted on the foreshore of The Pass by Arakwal Bundjalung woman Delta Kay from Explore Byron Bay is a must-do. Feel the spirituality of Walgun as you walk in the footsteps of Delta's ancestors. And don't forget to look up for Miwing, the white-bellied sea eagle, an important totem animal for Arakwal people that can often be spotted circling overhead, on the lookout for its next meal.

On the foreshore you'll also find the wheelchair-accessible Palm Valley Currenbah walking track, which makes a 0.3-mile (700m) loop through a serene, shaded palm rainforest, with picnic and barbecue facilities at either end. Now long gone, Byron's first permanent colonist dwelling was built in this very spot in 1882 or 1883.

You can also follow the incredibly scenic Cape Byron walking track from here to Australia's most easterly point; allow at least an hour to complete the 2.3-mile (3.7km) loop, which also takes in Wategos Beach – home to some of Australia's most exclusive real estate – and peaceful Little Wategos, accessible only by foot.

A rocky outcrop rises from the northern end of The Pass, with stairs leading up to a platform offering spectacular vistas

GETTING THERE

With limited paid parking at the beach, the scenic 20-minute walk along the sand from central Byron (or the wheelchair accessible pathway on the foreshore), is the best way to get to The Pass. There's also limited paid parking at neighbouring Captain Cook and Clarkes beaches.

from the Cape Byron Lighthouse to the east, around to the distinctive and culturally significant peak of Wollumbin (formerly Mount Warning) to the northwest. Below, rockpools dotted between the sharp rocks provide hours of fun for the young and young at heart.

While scoring a car park space at The Pass these days can feel like winning the lottery, it's still a magical beach to visit even on the most crowded summer days, with Wajung (dolphins, another important totem animal) often spotted riding waves alongside surfers. If you're planning to join them, ensure your board has a leg rope – in 2023, Byron Shire Council became the first in Australia to announce fines for surfing without a leash. Beginners can also take surf lessons here.

Sunset is a particularly special time at The Pass, when the sun sinks below Wollumbin, the sky erupts in a blaze of pinks and tangerines, and surfers chase the last waves of the day. Breathe deep and take it all in.

Bells Beach

SURF COAST, VICTORIA
AUSTRALIA

ONE OF AUSTRALIA'S most legendary surfing beaches, Bells was enshrined in pop culture when Patrick Swayze's adrenaline junkie character Bodhi waits his whole life to surf its fabled '50-year swell' in the 1991 action film *Point Break*. Never mind that the surfing scene was actually filmed in Oregon in the United States.

The red-clay cliffs framing this natural amphitheatre swell with spectators every Easter during the Rip Curl Pro Bells Beach, as the world's top surfers converge to carve up Bells' famous right-hand

point break. The longest-running event in competitive surfing, it's an iconic stop on the World Surf League Championship Tour. Australia's own Gail Cooper took out the title a whopping 10 times in the 1960s and '70s, with Aussies Mick Fanning and Stephanie Gilmore, as well as Kelly Slater and Lisa Andersen from the US each bagging four titles apiece to date.

Getting There
Located on Victoria's Great Ocean Road, Bells Beach is 3.1 miles (5km) from the closest town of Jan Juc, or a 90-minute drive southwest of Melbourne. You can also get here by bus. Stairs lead down from the car park to the small beach, which is best for swimming and casual surfing from November to March. Powerful swells served up by the Southern Ocean from April to October makes Bells best suited to experienced surfers during the cooler months.

Cable Beach/ Walmanyjun

BROOME, WESTERN AUSTRALIA
AUSTRALIA

A MAGNIFICENT SWEEP of blonde sand sandwiched between the turquoise waters of the Indian Ocean and the red pindan soil of the Kimberley, Cable Beach/Walmanyjun has earned its renown as Western Australia's most famous stretch of sand. Located in the former pearling port of Broome in the state's northwest, the 13.7-mile (22km) beach is synonymous with camels, sunset rides along the sand (or simply photographing them) being a highlight for many visitors. At the southern end, walking trails lead through the red dunes of Minyirr Park, a spiritual place for the Yawuru people, the region's Traditional Owners. The pindan cliffs of Gantheaume Point at Cable Beach's southern tip aren't just a pretty sight, they also guard one of Australia's most significant collections of dinosaur footprints, visible at low tide.

Cable Beach takes its name from the undersea telegraph cable from Java that came ashore there in 1899, which was used for international communications until 1914. The dry season (May to October) is the best time of the year to hit the beach, with beachgoers advised to avoid entering the water from November to April due to the presence of deadly Irukandji (Carukia barnesi) jellyfish, crocodiles and sharks. Cable Beach is patrolled by lifeguards daily from April to October.

GETTING THERE
Broome is 1243 miles (2000km) or a 2-hour-40-minute flight from Perth. It's a 30-minute walk from the town centre to Cable Beach, or you can take a bus or taxi.

Wineglass Bay

FREYCINET NATIONAL PARK, TASMANIA
AUSTRALIA

~~~~~~~~

A PHOTOGENIC ASSEMBLY of pink granite mountains, azure bays and rugged coastal forest, the Freycinet peninsula is a slice of heaven dangling off Tasmania's northeast coast. A perfect arc of powder-white sand framed by raw wilderness, its most celebrated feature is Wineglass Bay.

Grimly named for the scarlet shade its waters took on in the 1800s when whalers and sealers were active here, the now-protected bay is a much more agreeable hue today, with a ring of neon-turquoise water separating the porcelain sand from the indigo depths of the South Pacific.

The best view of the beach is from the Mt Amos Lookout, a strenuous 2.2-mile (3.6km) return scramble that takes around three hours. You can also admire Wineglass Bay by ascending the saddle between Mt Amos and Mt Mayson as far as the Wineglass Bay Lookout (one to 1½ hours return, 600 steps each way) or continue down the other side to the beach (2½ to three hours return). Look out for black cockatoos, Bennett's wallabies, dolphins and other critters on the way.

A 4.3-mile (7km) drive east of the national park's visitor centre at Coles Bay, the 0.3-mile (500m) wheelchair-friendly boardwalk at Cape Tourville affords sweeping coastal panoramas and a less-strenuous glimpse of Wineglass Bay.

~~~~~~~~

GETTING THERE
The national park is about a 2½ to three-hour drive from either Launceston or Hobart. On longer walks, sign in (and out) at the registration booth at the car park; national park fees apply. There's a small campsite and a composting toilet at the southern end of the beach.

Bondi Beach

SYDNEY, NEW SOUTH WALES
AUSTRALIA

~~~~~~

SYNONYMOUS WITH SYDNEY, Bondi Beach is so much more than half a mile (1km) of blonde sand bookended by golden sandstone cliffs. It's a cultural icon – the birthplace of the world's first surf-lifesaving organisation, formed in 1907, and the setting of countless films and television series including one of Australia's longest-running shows, *Bondi Rescue*.

The closest ocean beach to the city centre (4.3 miles/7km away), Bondi has azure water and consistently good waves for surfing, particularly at the southern end of the beach. The United Nations of beaches, Bondi hosts visitors from all corners of the city – and the world – particularly on summertime weekends, when beachgoers descend on its sands in their thousands.

If you've tuned into *Bondi Rescue*, which follows the action-packed days of Australia's busiest lifeguards, you'll know that swimming between the red-and-yellow flags is always a good idea. If the sea's looking a bit angry for you, just head to the child-friendly ocean baths at either end of the beach. At the southern end, the Bondi Icebergs turquoise pool is as iconic as the beach itself, famous for its hardy locals who can be seen making their daily laps year-round as waves crash over the edge. Perched on the cliffs above, Italian restaurant Icebergs Dining Room and Bar is one of Sydney's most popular lunch venues – keep a discreet eye out for celebrities. Beginning at the southern end of Bondi Beach, the 3.5-mile (6km) Bondi-to-Cogee coastal walk is another popular way to experience this glorious stretch of coastline.

At the northern end of Bondi there's a grassy spot with coin-operated barbecues, but don't bring alcohol to your picnic – it's prohibited on the beach. Smoking is also banned on all Waverly

~~~~~~

GETTING THERE
Take a train to Bondi Junction and transfer to any bus bound for Bondi Beach. The combined journey from the city centre by public transport takes around 45 minutes. Limited paid parking is also available at the beachfront and on surrounding streets.

Council beaches, including Bondi. Changing rooms and lockers can be found at the historic Bondi Pavilion in the middle of the park behind the beach, recently renovated with a range of new creative and dining spaces. Free beach-friendly wheelchairs (for adults and children) can also be booked through Bondi Pavilion. Looking for your LGBTQIA+ community? Head to North Bondi Surf Club, where an outdoor gym attracts a steady stream of buff bods and is one of the main hangouts for queer beach-going Sydneysiders.

The installation of shark nets off Bondi Beach remains a controversial topic, with nets across New South Wales entangling hundreds of non-target species each year. Bondi hasn't experienced a fatal shark encounter since 1929, though in 2022, it hit the headlines following the first shark-related fatality in Sydney's Eastern Beaches in almost 60 years. The tragedy occurred at Little Bay, around 6.2 miles (10km) south of Bondi as the crow flies (or the shark swims). Drownings at Bondi and other Australian beaches are sadly far more common, with around 50 nationally each summer. While sharks continue to make the odd appearance at Bondi, you're more likely to spot bottlenose dolphins dancing in the surf. From May to November, keep an eye out for humpback whales breaching off the coast during their annual migration.

Lucky Bay/ Kepa Kurl

CAPE LE GRAND NATIONAL PARK/ MANDOOWERNUP, WESTERN AUSTRALIA
AUSTRALIA

~~~

IMAGINE SAND SO WHITE and so fine it whistles underfoot, and water in shades of blue so beautiful it's impossible to resist. Cradle it between scenic granite outcrops linked by bushwalking trails and add a few kangaroos, and you have Lucky Bay.

Stretching for 12.4 miles (20km), this protected bay near Esperance in the state's southwest is right up there with Australia's dreamiest. Float in the crystalline water, cast a line at a secluded fishing spot, or gaze out to the ocean for the chance to see migrating whales between July and October. From November to early March, consistently windy days make the shallow bay popular with kitesurfers.

Come for the day or pack a tent and camp under a moonlit sky at the western end of the beach, keeping in mind that the 56 spots in this Cape Le Grand National Park campground can book out in advance. Tame kangaroos are most commonly sighted on and around the beach at dawn and dusk; resist the urge to touch or feed them.

~~~

GETTING THERE
Lucky Bay is 39.8 miles (64km), or a 50-minute drive, east of Esperance, which is another 435-mile (700km) drive (or a short flight) from Perth. There is no public transport to Lucky Bay.

Squeaky Beach

GIPPSLAND, VICTORIA
AUSTRALIA

ENCLOSED BY IMPRESSIVE granite boulders at either end, Squeaky Beach is a standout in Wilsons Promontory National Park, an awe-inspiring slice of wilderness at the southernmost tip of mainland Australia, fringed by Victoria's largest marine national park. The fine, rounded grains of quartz sand on this snow-white beach compress under your feet, creating a high-pitched squeak – hence the name. Wander between the huge boulders at the northern end of the beach and splash in hidden rock pools, or dive into the bay's crystalline waters, which are at their most inviting during the warmer months (particularly November to March). Connecting Squeaky Beach with Picnic Bay and Whisky Bay to the north, the 3.9-mile (6.2km) Three Bays Walk is an invigorating way to experience this spectacular stretch of coastline. Allow two hours each way.

There's camping close by at Tidal River, just back from neighbouring Norman Beach, offering the perfect opportunity to savour a mesmerising Squeaky Beach sunset. Native wildlife-watching opportunities also increase during the golden hour – keep an eye out for wombats, kangaroos, emus and more.

GETTING THERE

Squeaky Beach is 138 miles (222km) or an approximately three-hour drive from Melbourne. Park behind the beach or walk here from Picnic Bay or Tidal River. Alternatively, catch a Yarram-bound bus to Fish Creek, and take a taxi from there.

Tangalooma Beach

MORETON ISLAND/ MULGUMPIN, QUEENSLAND
AUSTRALIA

~~~~~

THE THIRD-LARGEST SAND ISLAND in the world, Moreton Island/Mulgumpin is an idyll of blonde sandy beaches, rolling dunes, native bushland and serene lagoons some 35.4 miles (57km) off the coast of Brisbane. With 95% of the isle protected by the Moreton Island National Park and Recreation Area, it's a sublime spot to unplug by the sea near Queensland's capital.

Fringing the island's protected west coast, the long, narrow strip of sand known as Tangalooma Beach feels a world away from the city, backed by bushland and lapped by calm turquoise waters frequented by dolphins, turtles, rays and elusive dugongs. Just off the shallow beach, the rusty, hulking Tangalooma Wrecks are the top attraction. Scuttled over two decades from the 1960s to create a safe anchorage for boat owners, the 15 wrecks are now encrusted with corals that attract plenty of fish, making for excellent snorkelling. Shallow diving is also possible here.

Nestled in bushland just behind the beach is one of five basic campsites (and additional camping zones) on the island. There is more accommodation at the southern end of the beach, including a resort. You'll need 4WD to access campsites beyond Tangalooma, as the island's 'roads' are sand tracks.

~~~~~

GETTING THERE
Four daily passenger ferry services (75 minutes) depart from Holt Street Wharf in Pinkenba, Brisbane, and arrive at the Tangalooma Jetty on Moreton Island. A car ferry runs on demand from the Port of Brisbane. Or you can visit on a day cruise from Brisbane.

Whitehaven Beach

WHITSUNDAYS, QUEENSLAND
AUSTRALIA

THE SWIRLING PATTERN of aquamarine water and snow-white sandbars at the northern end of Whitehaven Beach – officially called Hill Inlet – is one of Australia's most photogenic natural icons. And when you sink your toes into the 98% pure silica sands of this dazzling beach in Queensland's Whitsunday Islands National Park, you'll understand the hype. Framed by the sparkling Coral Sea and the lush vegetation of uninhabited and essentially untouched Whitsunday Island, the 4.3-mile-long (7km) beach on the traditional lands of the Ngaro people is quite simply magical. Most day trips from neighbouring Hamilton Island and the mainland backpacker hub of Airlie Beach include stops on Whitehaven Beach and the northern side of Hill Inlet, where you can (and should) take a 0.8-mile (1.3km) return bushwalk to twin lookouts for mesmerizing views across the inlet. Day trips often include snorkelling stops at local fringing reefs forming part of the Great Barrier Reef Marine Park, but the coral and visibility tends to be better on the outer reef. Don't miss a chance to dive in for a swim here, though, with the water sitting at a delightful average temperature of 79°F (26°C) year-round. Whitehaven's ultra-fine white sand – its origin continuing to baffle geologists – also makes a great exfoliant.

GETTING THERE

Whitehaven Beach is a 30-minute catamaran ride from Hamilton Island, and about one hour on a high-speed boat from Airlie Beach, 15.5 miles (25km) to the west. Helicopter and seaplane tours are available for those in search of the perfect aerial shot. Boats are permitted to anchor in Hill Inlet and off Whitehaven Beach, and there's a basic national park campground at the southern end of the beach.

Africa

ABOVE Le Morne Beach and
the island of Mauritius.
LEFT Anse Source d'Argent in
the dazzling Seychelles.

Camps Bay Beach

CAPE TOWN, WESTERN CAPE
SOUTH AFRICA

WITH SOFT WHITE SAND and a backdrop of the craggy Twelve Apostles range (part of Table Mountain), it's easy to see why this Blue Flag beach is one of Cape Town's most popular. On weekends crowds from all over the city descend on its sands, giving the beach a lively party atmosphere, particularly during the peak months of December and January. While summer days can heat up to 86°F (30°C), the azure water tends to be on the chilly side year-round. When the swell turns on (typically in autumn), experienced surfers will find powerful, hollow waves at the northern end of the bay, known as Glen Beach.

With a strip of restaurants and bars right across the street, you can hop over to grab a quick bite or drink before heading back to the sand. It's worth checking the wind forecast before you pack your beach bag, as it can get quite blustery here.

GETTING THERE
MyCity buses 107 and 118 both run from downtown Cape Town to
Camps Bay Beach, 4.3 miles (7km) to the southwest. If you're driving,
you can park alongside the beach on Victoria Rd – if you can find a spot.

Mnemba Island

ZANZIBAR
TANZANIA

THERE'S NOTHING LIKE A FEW DAYS relaxing on the tropical white-sand beaches of Zanzibar to top off an action-packed safari holiday on mainland Tanzania. While many visitors flock to the wide, hotel-lined beaches of Nungwi and Kendwa on the northern shores of Unguja, there are plenty of other similarly seductive – yet far less crowded – beaches fringing the main island of this intriguing Indian Ocean archipelago. For a special treat, cast away from Zanzibar's north-east coast for exclusive access to the ravishing ring of sand skirting Mnemba Island as a guest of the resort &BEYOND Mnemba Island.

Here you'll share the tiny island's unblemished sands with a maximum of just 23 fellow guests. Enjoy a leisurely walk around the island as crabs scuttle across the sparkling sand and seabirds ride the breeze, lean into the simple luxury of unwinding on your private beachfront deck shaded by casuarina trees, or dive into the aquamarine water to enjoy some of the best snorkelling and scuba diving in Africa's spice islands.

GETTING THERE

Rates include transfers by car from Stone Town or Zanzibar's airport to Muyuni Beach, followed by a short boat transfer ride to Mnemba Island.

Le Morne Beach

BLACK RIVER
MAURITIUS

A NARROW SLIVER OF BLONDE SAND fringed by a vast turquoise lagoon and backed by the impressive basalt hulk of Le Morne Brabant, Le Morne is an absolute showstopper. Better yet, it's also a public beach; its shallow lagoon curling around the western tip of Mauritius luring kitesurfers from all corners of the globe when the wind picks up between April and November.

Le Morne is also a Unesco site – but it wasn't inscribed for its natural beauty. Through the 18th and early 19th centuries, escaped enslaved people known as maroons formed communities in the caves and on the summit of Le Morne Brabant. A testimony to the resistance of slavery, Le Morne is now a symbol of the maroons' fight for freedom, their suffering and their sacrifice. As you pull into the public beach car park, you'll spot the Slave Route Monument across the road. It's a powerful reminder that Mauritius isn't just a beautiful beach destination, but also a rich cultural landscape with many stories to tell.

It's possible to hike to the top of Le Morne Brabant (1824ft/ 556m); allow three-to-four hours return, with a scramble to the top – worth it for the mesmerising views.

GETTING THERE
Le Morne Beach is 34.8 miles (56km) or just over an hour-long drive west of Sir Seewoosagur Ramgoolam International Airport. It takes roughly the same time to drive from Le Morne to the capital Port Louis to the north.

Nosy Iranja

MADAGASCAR

A NARROW STRIP of gleaming white sand connects the twin islands of Nosy Iranja Be and tiny, uninhabited Nosy Iranja Kely, just off Madagascar's northwestern coast. Possibly the world's most idyllic sandbar, this one-mile-long (1.6km) beach rising out of the tropical turquoise water is a popular day trip from the larger resort island of Nosy Be to the northeast, with excursions generally including snorkelling, swimming and a tasty seafood lunch prepared by the crew. There is usually enough

time during a day trip for active visitors to trace the length of the sandbar on foot, as well as hike up a hill on Nosy Iranja Be for a magnificent view of the beach snaking its way across the glittering western Indian Ocean towards Nosy Iranja Kely.

Enjoy this slice of paradise for a little longer by overnighting on Nosy Iranja Be, which has a bungalow-style hotel as well as rustic beach hut accommodation.

GETTING THERE

Nosy Iranja is around 25 miles (40km) from Nosy Be. The trip takes about an hour by speed-boat, but with tour boats tending to pause for tourists to view dolphins and turtles en route, it usually takes longer.

Anse Source d'Argent

LA DIGUE
SEYCHELLES

IT REGULARLY TOPS world's best beach lists, but does Anse Source d'Argent live up to the hype? In a word: yes. Stretching along the southwestern coast of La Digue, the fourth-largest island in the Seychelles, its dazzling white sands are lapped by shallow turquoise waters, backed by some of La Digue's most beautiful granite boulders and shaded by craning coconut palms.

Part of the fun is getting here. First you'll need to catch a ferry to La Digue, which doesn't have an airport, then walk or hire a rickety bicycle to pedal 1.2 miles (2km) south to L'Union Estate, a former vanilla and coconut plantation that charges a small entry fee to access the beach on its land. Here you can pause to tour the planter's house (now a museum), wander the historic cemetery, and check out the Aldabra giant tortoise pen. The road continues through a picturesque coconut palm plantation to the entrance to the beach, another 0.43 miles (700m) south. Here you'll spot the jumping-off point for Crystal Water Kayaks tours, which offer a stunning perspective on the beach from the seat of a transparent kayak. Nearby, the island-style Lanboursir Restaurant is the closest place to the beach to get a feed.

Follow the sandy path around a cluster of boulders to get your first glimpse of heaven on Earth. Sculped by the wind and waves over millennia, the smooth granite boulders spilling onto the beach look more like works of art. Towards the end of the 0.3-mile-long (500m) stretch of sand, you'll find a twin set of rustic beach bars selling fresh fruit juices and fresh coconuts, which you can (and should) opt to enjoy with a shot of local Takamaka rum. Then all that's left to do is swim, laze, snap, repeat. Yes, pack that extra camera battery.

At low tide you can pick your way around the boulders at the southern end of the beach to find a string of smaller bays. If you're feeling energetic, it's possible to hike from here to the small, secluded and similarly beautiful Anse Marron at the southern tip of the island. With the route including some boulder scrambling and trekking along unmarked jungle tracks, it's a sweaty, full-day adventure best attempted with a local guide – and an adequate supply of drinking water and snacks.

Anse Source d'Argent is justifiably popular, so the sands can get crowded, particularly as the beach area shrinks at high tide. Coming in the early morning and returning in the late afternoon is a great way to avoid many of the island's day visitors (keep your entrance ticket). As the sun starts to descend you can relax on the sand and feel like you have this uninhabited piece of paradise all to yourself.

There are multiple daily ferries to La Digue from Praslin, but with plenty of accommodation on La Digue, it's worth spending a few days here to explore the island and soak up its deliciously laid-back vibe.

GETTING THERE
It takes less than two hours to reach La Digue by ferry from Victoria on the main island of Mahé, and just 15 minutes by ferry from Baie Ste Anne in Praslin.

Asia

LEFT A perfect day for a swim
at Sunayama Beach, Japan.
TOP The perfectly pink sand at
Pink Beach, Indonesia.

Radhanagar

SWARAJ DWEEP, ANDAMAN ISLANDS
INDIA

~~~

IN ONE OF INDIA'S most blissfully secluded corners, a glinting sweep of pale-blonde, flour-soft sand disappears into the hazy distance, backed by a swirl of electric-green forest made up of ancient, endemic species found nowhere else on Earth. Most evenings, people gather here and chat away as the sun's blazing coral hues bounce off the aqua waves before it sinks into the Andaman Sea. This is Radhanagar, the almost-mythical beach that is putting India's remote, wildly beautiful Andaman Islands on the map. Hugging the northwest coast of mellow Swaraj Dweep (formerly Havelock Island), it feels almost like a distant, tropical dream. People come to Swaraj Dweep for some of the finest diving and snorkelling in India (and indeed Asia), but you'll be just as entranced by the island's raw natural beauty. In past decades, some of the Andamans' famous ocean-swimming elephants were often spotted at Radhanagar and other local beaches – Rajan, who passed away in 2016 at age 66, was the last of his kind, but you might spot an elephant strolling along the shoreline.

~~~

GETTING THERE
The isolated Andaman Islands sit almost 870 miles (1400km) east of mainland India, so getting here is part of the adventure. Fly into Port Blair (the small regional capital, on South Andaman), then catch a two-hour ferry to Swaraj Dweep. Radhanagar awaits on the island's northwest coast, with a couple of eco-luxe resorts hidden among the trees.

Palolem Beach

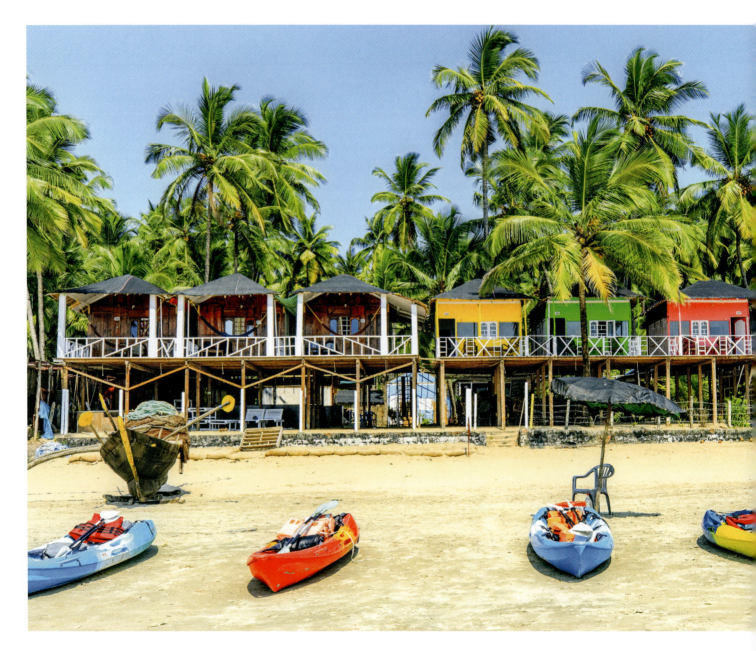

GETTING THERE

Palolem is 37 miles (60km) south of Goa's Dabolim Airport, which has plenty of domestic flights and a few international routes. It's also possible to reach Palolem by train from Indian destinations such as Mumbai (12½ hours) and Margao (Magdaon; 30 minutes), hopping off at Canacona station just 1.2 miles (2km) away, and there are plenty of local buses.

© Guzel Gashgullina / Shutterstock

GOA'S LUSCIOUS PALM-BACKED BEACHES are undoubtedly India's loveliest, but it's down in the sultry south – near the border with Karnataka – that you'll catch a real taste of this small sun-washed state's tranquil side. It doesn't get more blissfully South Goa than laid-back Palolem, where vibrant-green coconut palms ripple in the tropical breeze and a golden 1.2-mile (2km) crescent moon of sand extends along an irresistibly calm jade-tinged bay. Every high season (November to March), candy-coloured beach huts spring to life all along Palolem's shore, hosting everything from low-key guest rooms with swaying hammocks to buzzy thatched-roof restaurants serving Goan-style thalis and deliciously spiced fish curries. Stretch into the day with a beachfront yoga class, hire a kayak or a stand-up paddleboard to explore the protected coastline, or just laze on the sand and look out for dolphins frolicking on the horizon. Thanks to its slightly sheltered location, this is one of the best spots in Goa for a dip in the Arabian Sea, with the water here resting at around 79°F (26°C) most of the year.

Papanasham Beach

VARKALA, KERALA

INDIA

HEMMED IN BY DISTINCTIVE rust-red laterite cliffs, just north of Thiruvananthapuram (Trivandrum) in serene southern Kerala, Varkala's sun-toasted beaches are the stuff of tropical dreams. Salty-haired surfers catch swells in the bath-warm Arabian Sea, which rolls onto golden sands beneath 49ft-tall (15m) crags stretching along the palm-studded coast. This a place for soaking up South India's laid-back beach vibe, catching the sunset with your toes curled into the sand, learning all about ayurvedic therapies, and devouring super-fresh seafood and spiced masala dosas at the lively clifftop restaurants.

The main beach, Papanasham, is always a hive of activity – for Hindus, Varkala remains a major pilgrimage destination, and bathing in the holy waters here is believed to wash away sins. After clambering down cliffside stairs past lush greenery, you're greeted by a one-mile (1.6km) stretch of velvety sand where local kids frolic in the water, brightly painted fishing boats gather, international travellers laze under candy-coloured umbrellas, priests assist pilgrims with waterside rituals and yogis stretch into the day with ocean views. The revered, banyan-shaded Janardhana Temple, whose roots date back to the 13th century, sits a few hundred metres inland from Papanasam. Though the main shrine is closed to non-Hindus, visitors are welcome to wander the grounds.

As India's surf world continues its upward swing, Varkala's own surf scene has also blossomed in recent years, with keen surfers from other Indian hubs and beyond bringing the art of riding the waves to this small fishing town. Beach clean-ups, local-focused surf camps and other initiatives are all part of the picture. For

GETTING THERE
Varkala is 31 miles (50km) north-west of Kerala's capital Thiruvananthapuram (Trivandrum), which has an international airport. It's an easy one-hour train ride from Thiruvananthapuram to Varkala town, 1.2 miles (2km) inland from Papanasham Beach and with plenty of other rail links. Another option is to fly into the international airport at Kochi (Cochin), from where it's a 3½-hour train south to Varkala.

anyone looking to dive in, plenty of Varkala-based schools now offer surf retreats, courses and board rentals. Whatever your expertise level, the sight of those towering ochre cliffs from out on the azure water feels magical.

Those keen for a little more seclusion should head to the pretty coves just north of Varkala proper, such as gold-tinged Odayam Beach, or further afield to undeveloped Kappil Beach, which is fringed by meandering backwaters and makes a popular surf spot. Then there are yoga and meditation sessions overlooking the sea; sky-high paragliding excursions with birds-eye views; and kayaking and stand-up paddleboarding routes meandering along the coastline. Even just strolling along the curving clifftop pathways high above Papanasham, as the evening sun burns hot-pink over the glistening waves, is unforgettable. It's easy to see how people pop into Varkala for a day or two and end up staying for weeks.

White Sandy Beach

FULHADHOO ISLAND, NORTHERN ATOLLS
MALDIVES

IN AN ARCHIPELAGO blessed with thousands of idyllic white-sand beaches, it's difficult to play favourites. But if we had to choose one, it might just be the aptly named White Sandy Beach on the southwestern edge of Fulhadhoo Island. A long, narrow slick of blinding white sand nestling between naturally occurring tropical greenery and the cyan sea, the beach's castaway vibes are strong.

Facilities on the beach are few, save a handful of sunbeds shaded by bamboo canopies. Get here early and you can watch local fisherman – who live in a small village on the eastern edge of the island – as they bring in the night's catch. There are a handful of places to stay in the village, from luxury to budget. Unlike most of the resort islands in the Maldives, Fulhadhoo offers a taste of local life and culture along with its glorious beaches. Respect local customs by wearing a cover-up over swimwear in the village.

Next-door to Fulhadhoo, the uninhabited islands of Fehendhoo and Goidho proffer more beautiful beaches to explore.

GETTING THERE
Fulhadhoo Island is around 62.1 miles (100km) northwest from the capital Malé. Daily scheduled (and private) speedboat transfers take around 70 minutes. The cheaper, thrice-weekly ferry takes 3½ hours.

Pink Beach

PADAR ISLAND,
KOMODO NATIONAL PARK
INDONESIA

CANDY-PINK SANDS fizzle into turquoise seas at Komodo National Park's Pink Beach, thought to be one of only a handful of its kind in the world. The pretty beach's distinctive rosy blush comes courtesy of scarlet-red organ pipe corals that thrive offshore. Over centuries, broken coral fragments have mixed with the fine white sand, producing the soft pink hue visible along the shoreline.

On remote Padar Island, Pink Beach is a popular stop on Komodo island-hopping day trips from the tourism hub of Labuan

Bajo on the East Nusa Tenggara island of Flores. But there's more to this beach than its stunning sands, with some beautiful corals and plenty of tropical fish for snorkellers to admire just off the northern end of the beach. You might struggle to spot organ pipe corals, however, as their red skeletons are typically obscured by polyps with feathery tentacles that live in the tops of the pipe-like tubes.

A handful of simple beach huts offer drinks and simple meals as well as shade – there are no trees on this rather barren strip of sand.

GETTING THERE

On the northwest shore of Padar Island, around 24.9 miles (40km) from Labuan Bajo, Pink Beach can only be visited on a day tour from Labuan Bajo, or a private or multi-day liveaboard cruise.

Diamond Beach

NUSA PENIDA, BALI
INDONESIA

JUST A 35-MINUTE BOAT RIDE from neighbouring Bali, the mountainous island of Nusa Penida is encircled by the kind of jaw-dropping beaches that travellers may expect to discover on Bali but struggle to find. Top billing goes to Diamond Beach on the island's southeast shore – like most of the beaches on this side of the island, it's encased by soaring limestone cliff walls that turn the snow-white beach into a secluded cove. In fact, this remote curl of sand only became accessible to visitors after a rough staircase was, quite literally, carved out of the rock in 2018. Look out for manta rays dancing across the turquoise bay below as you set up the perfect snap, then head down to the beach for a refreshing dip on a calm day – swimming is not advised in rough swells. There's a small *warung* (basic restaurant) on the beach selling snacks.

With the development of tourism facilities, including effective waste management, yet to catch up to the popularity of Nusa Penida's clifftop beaches, it's particularly important not to leave any rubbish behind.

GETTING THERE
Day trips by boat and car are possible from Bali and the Nusa Penida sister-islands of Nusa Lembongan and Nusa Ceningan, but it's a more pleasant experience to stay on Nusa Penida, rent a scooter, and hit Diamond Beach (a 90-minute ride from the ferry dock) before the day trippers arrive from mid-morning.

Titop Beach

HALONG BAY, QUANG NINH

VIETNAM

~~~

TOWERING LIMESTONE PILLARS and tiny islets draped by lush forest rise from the emerald waters of Unesco-listed Halong Bay, a vision of ethereal beauty and, unsurprisingly, northern Vietnam's number one tourism hub.

Among the bay's many natural treasures is Titop (also known as Titov) Beach, a small crescent of white sand clinging to its tiny namesake island. Named by former president Ho Chi Minh for the Russian cosmonaut Gherman Stepanovich Titov, it's one of few beaches in the archipelago, with a boat dock at its eastern end and a designated swimming area in the middle of the beach designed to keep paddlers out of harm's way. Active visitors can climb the thigh-burning set of stairs to the summit (360ft/110m above sea level) for mesmerising views across the bay before diving into the bay to cool off, or rehydrating with a fresh coconut water purchased from one of the beach stalls.

GETTING THERE

Titop can be visited on a day or overnight cruise from Tuan Chau Harbour, outside Halong City, both of which also visit other Halong Bay highlights on their itineraries. Frequent shuttles run from Hanoi to the port.

Pacifico Beach

SIARGAO, SURIGAO DEL NORTE
PHILIPPINES

THE LUSH, TEARDROP-SHAPED ISLE of Siargao was something of a surfers' secret until relatively recently. It's not only the hollow barrels of surf town General Luna's legendary Cloud 9 break that put this blissfully low-key isle on the travel map, but also its azure, coconut palm-shaded beaches like Pacifico. Lapped by a protected turquoise lagoon studded with patches of emerald seagrass that give the water its dreamy, mottled hue, this scythe of white sand is a textbook tropical fantasy. There's also a left-hand reef break if you don't mind a bit of a paddle across the lagoon.

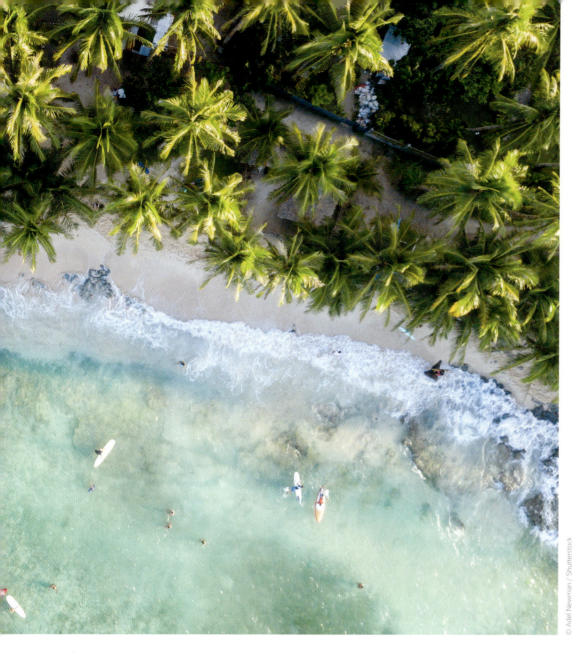

In December 2021, a powerful typhoon essentially flattened Siargao, including the then-fledgling surf town of Pacifico on the island's secluded northeast coast. The devastated island staged an incredible comeback, with many homes and businesses, including a handful of places to stay and eat in Pacifico, rebuilt and reopened within a year. With tourism continuing to play a key role in the island's ongoing recovery, there's no better time to experience its magic for yourself.

GETTING THERE

Pacifico Beach is 13 miles (21km) or a 30-minute drive north of Surigao's domestic airport, or 31 miles (50km) north of the island's main tourism hub of General Luna. The drive from the latter, typically undertaken by rental scooter, takes just over an hour, but most visitors take all day to get here, with plenty of viewpoints and other attractions worth a detour on the way.

Maremegmeg Beach

EL NIDO, PALAWAN
PHILIPPINES

AS THE SUN DIPS BEHIND the jungle-shrouded karst islands dotting serene Baciut Bay, travellers scuttle, piña coladas in hand, to the western tip of Maremegmeg Beach (often referred to as Las Cabanas Beach) to catch one of the most dazzling sunsets on the island (and province) of Palawan. Tangerine beams light up their smiling faces, and you can't just hear the collective sigh of content, you can feel it.

In a region blessed with hundreds – perhaps thousands – of gorgeous turquoise beaches backed by soaring cliffs, this thin strip of sand scores extra points for its easy-to-access location, just 3.1 miles (5km) or a 15-minute scooter ride from the busy tourism hub of El Nido. Lined by a handful of casual restaurants and bars, and low-key resorts, there's no shortage of places to stay and play in between refreshing dips in the sea. While ever-increasing development in the area hasn't dimmed its appeal yet, Maremegmeg is one of those beaches worth visiting sooner rather than later.

GETTING THERE

Maremegmeg Beach is 6.2 miles (10km) or a 20-minute drive south of the domestic El Nido Airport, and 163.4 miles (263km) or a 4½-hour drive north of Palawan's Puerto Princesa International Airport.

Secret Beach

MIRISSA, MATARA DISTRICT
SRI LANKA

WEST OF THE MAIN BEACH in Mirissa, a popular surfing destination on Sri Lanka's southwestern coast, Secret Beach is the perfect name for this tiny wedge of white sand flanked by jungle-covered hills. With next to no development other than a rustic beach bar tucked beneath the coconut palms, this sweet slice of the coast isn't exactly a secret, but it still feels like one.

Actually two tiny curves of golden sand that meet at a small rocky outcrop, Secret Beach features a serene tidal lagoon perfect for a lazy swim on its western side, with the eastern side offering easier access to the sparkling Indian Ocean through a larger gap in the rocky shoreline. With five out of the world's seven species of sea turtles frequenting Sri Lanka's waters, keep your eyes peeled if you go for a snorkel (masks as well as beach chairs can be rented at the beach bar).

GETTING THERE
Mirissa is 105.6 miles (170km) southeast of the capital Colombo. Trains and buses run here from the capital. Secret Beach is a half-mile (0.8km) walk downhill from Mirissa's Port on Harbour Road. It's easier to get here on a rental scooter.

Hat Tham Phra Nang

RAILAY, KRABI
THAILAND

KRABI'S FAIRY-TALE LIMESTONE FORMATIONS come to a dramatic climax at Railay, the ultimate Andaman gym for rock-climbing fanatics. Monkeys frolic alongside climbers on the gorgeous crags, while down below some of the prettiest beaches in Thailand are backed by verdant jungle. A crescent of pale golden sand, framed by soaring karst cliffs and Ko Kai (Chicken Island) and Ko Poda peeking out of the cerulean sea, Hat Tham Phra Nang is the finest of them all.

Sandwiched between the not-good-for-swimming beach of Hat Railay East and the resorts of nicer Hat Railay West, Hat Tham

Phra Nang is a vision of paradise. At the eastern end of the beach is a popular climbing spot and an important shrine for local fisher-folk (Muslim and Buddhist), who make offerings of carved wooden phalluses in the hope that the inhabiting spirit of a drowned Indian princess will provide a good catch. There are plenty of shady spots along the idyllic beach, but no facilities, so you'll need to walk back along the jungle path to Hat Railay East or West for food and drinks if you don't bring your own.

GETTING THERE

Only accessible by boat, Railay is a 15-minute trip from Ao Nang. Multiple daily boats also run from Phuket, Krabi Town and Ko Phi-Phi Don. Spend the night in Railay to enjoy the tranquillity when the day-tripping crowds depart.

Ao Maya

KO PHI-PHI LEH, KRABI
THAILAND

WITH ITS DRAMATIC KARST CLIFFS, fine white sand and cyan bay, Ao Maya (Maya Bay), part of the Hat Noppharat Thara-Mu Ko Phi-Phi National Park, meets even Hollywood's standards for a tropical paradise. In 1999, its beautiful sands were controversially used as a film set for the Leonardo di Caprio-starring blockbuster *The Beach*, based on Alex Garland's novel, and the site quickly became a pilgrimage of sorts for travellers who flocked here following the film's release the following year.

Just 49ft-wide (15m) and 820ft-long (250m), the relatively small beach on uninhabited Ko Phi-Phi Leh became a victim of its own popularity, with an estimated 6000 people visiting the picturesque cove each day by 2018. Visitors left behind rubbish, damaged plants and sand, and spooked wildlife, and boat anchors are thought to have destroyed as much as 50% of Ao Maya's coral. Images of thousands of tourists thronging what was ostensibly a protected natural area led to outrage among Thais, and in 2018, park officials abruptly closed the bay in an effort to combat the damage.

Initially, the closure was meant to last four months. But realising that it would take much longer for the ecosystem to recover, and to install the infrastructure required to protect it, officials gradually extended the freeze to four years. Ao Maya finally reopened on 1 January 2022, shortly after Thailand reopened to vaccinated tourists in the wake of the pandemic.

After the entrance to Ao Maya was barricaded in 2018, the bay was thoroughly cleaned of rubbish and revegetation works commenced above and below the water, with more than 30,000 pieces of coral planted in the bay's decimated reefs. Next, work began on installing new tourism infrastructure including a floating dock located behind the karst cliffs, a beach-access boardwalk, bathrooms and a cafe.

Ao Maya reopened with new rules. Boats are no longer allowed to anchor in the bay, visitor numbers are capped at 375 people per hour-long slot, and swimming in the bay is now banned, with visitors only allowed to wade in as deep as knee-height.

Yet feedback from visitors – especially returning beachgoers – has been overwhelmingly positive, with many agreeing that the strict measures are worth it to admire this paradisical bay in a more natural state, free of boats blocking the iconic vista from the sand. From particular angles, it appears as though the bay is completely enclosed from the open sea by the jungle-encrusted cliffs surrounding it (there's actually an opening of about 984ft/300m).

Ao Maya's closure appeared to benefit the natural environment – at least initially, with an underwater camera allowing scientists to count blacktip sharks returning in droves shortly after the initial closure. But with conservationists reporting that shark numbers are thinning out again, it's evident that striking a balance between preserving the ecosystem and sustaining livelihoods dependent on tourism remains a challenge for Ao Maya. Most people would agree that this famous beach is at least on the right track.

GETTING THERE

Day trips by speedboat from Phuket and Krabi are possible, but for the best experience, stay on neighbouring Ko Phi-Phi Don and take an early morning boat tour here (20 minutes each way) to beat the bulk of the crowds.

Secret Beach

TRANG ISLANDS, TRANG
THAILAND

EXTENDING IN A SPLENDID ARC down Thailand's far southern Andaman coast, the glittering Trang Islands offer a wonderful step up in tranquility from their well-trodden neighbours to the north. Here jaunty rock formations rise from sparkling emerald waters, sugary beaches wrap jungle-shrouded hills, speedboats buzz between road-free islands and weathered long-tail boats putter around with a refreshing lack of urgency.

Situated inside Hat Chao Mai National Park, which has kept development on the islands to a minimum, the jewel in the archipelago is Ko Kradan. Visitors stay in low-rise bungalows and resorts on east-facing Kradan Beach – also known as Paradise Beach, this skinny, palm-fringed strip is perfectly lovely. But perhaps the island's prettiest beach is tiny Sunset Beach on the west coast, reached by a short jungle hike or by longtail boat – there are no roads on the island. The beach's name says it all: go at the end of the day to watch the sky flare into magenta, turmeric and scarlet hues. Bring a torch (flashlight) for the walk back through the jungle in the darkness.

GETTING THERE
The most convenient way for most travellers to get to Ko Kradan is to take one of the twice-daily fast ferries from Ko Lanta. The journey takes around an hour.

Sunayama Beach

MIYAKOJIMA ISLAND, OKINAWA

JAPAN

NO, YOU'RE NOT TECHNICALLY in the tropics. But you can be forgiven for thinking you are in Okinawa's Southwest Islands. Lying at the bottom of a large sand dune (hence the name 'Sand Mountain Beach'), Sunayama Beach is among the archipelago's finest coves, with snow-white sands and a dramatic arch at its southern end, formed by the erosion of an exposed coral reef over centuries. Accessed via a short, sandy pathway slicing through a thicket of verdant greenery fringing the beach, petite Sunayama feels like a secret. But lucky is the traveller who has the pleasure of enjoying this popular spot all to themselves.

The region's azure waters lure scuba divers aplenty, and while the reefs directly off this beach aren't a particular highlight, snorkellers can still expect to spot a variety of fish on calm days. If you've only got one beach day to spend in the region, this is the place to park yourself.

GETTING THERE

Sunayama Beach lies just 2.5 miles (4km) north of the Hirara district of Miyakojima city. Renting a car is a popular way to explore the island, but it's also possible to access the beach by taxi and local bus.

Middle East

ABOVE The sand and the sea
(and the Hilton) as seen from
above Fuwairit Kite Beach, Qatar.
RIGHT The spectacular stretch
of sand at Qalansiyah Beach,
Yemen.

Fuwairit Kite Beach

AL SHAMAL
QATAR

THE STARK QATARI DESERT meets the crystal-blue waters of the Arabian Gulf at Fuwairit Kite Beach, the most pleasant spot for a swim on the coastline that almost entirely encircles the Arab state of Qatar. At least outside of the kitesurfing (read: windy) season from January to June, when kiters from all over the world descend on Fuwairit to slice across its clear, shallow waters – a sight to behold from the sand.

Until very recently, this lonely stretch of coastline was completely undeveloped, save for a handful of private compounds and the crumbling remains of several fishing villages, which were abandoned when Qatar's oil and gas industries took off in the mid-20th century. A brightly decorated Hilton-branded resort right on the beach now offers the only place to stay and eat at Fuwairit.

If you're not using the resort facilities, you'll need to bring everything with you for a day on the beach, including adequate sun protection and drinking water. The months of April and October are generally the best for swimming, when it's not too hot in or out of the water. From May to August, the shallow sea can feel like a warm bath. From April to July, the northern section of the beach, which forms a peninsula, is typically closed off to protect nesting hawksbill turtles.

GETTING THERE

Fuwairit Beach is 59 miles (95km) or about an hour-long drive from the capital Doha. There are no direct buses, but you can catch a bus to Al Khor, just over halfway, and get a taxi from there.

Mahmya Beach

GIFTUN ISLANDS, RED SEA GOVERNATE
EGYPT

JUST A 20-MINUTE boat ride from the Red Sea resort of
Hurghada, Mahmya Beach is a vision of blue – a palette of turquoise and cerulean so dreamy you might need to pinch yourself.
The most picturesque beach on the desert island of Giftun Kebir
(Big Giftun), its blonde sands are anchored by the confusingly
named Mahmya Island beach club, which offers superb views from
its shaded sunbeds across a deep channel towards Giftun Sughayer
(Little Giftun). Day visits include transfers from Hurghada, beach
chair use and a towel, with the option to add a buffet or a la carte
lunch. Snorkels, kayaks and stand-up paddleboards can be rented,
and beach volleyball is free. It's a glorious day out, but don't expect
a completely Zen experience, with banana boats zooming across
the beach's calm, shallow waters throughout the day. Some snorkelling day trips from Hurghada stop at Mahmya Beach.

    National park status has helped to deter development on the
Giftun Islands beyond Giftun Kebir's handful of beach clubs. With
any luck, it'll stay that way.

GETTING THERE

Mahmya Beach is only accessible by boat. Book a visit through Mahmya, or a travel agency in Hurghada. There is not currently anywhere to stay overnight on the island.

Qalansiyah Beach

QALANSIYAH, SOCOTRA
YEMEN

SOME 217.5 MILES (350KM) SOUTH of the Arabian Peninsula, Socotra belongs politically to Yemen but is geographically a part of Africa. A Unesco World Heritage site since 2008, the main island's rugged, blistered interior shelters remarkable diversity: more than 700 of the island's species (including one-third of Socotra's plant species) are found nowhere else on Earth. Geographers consider Socotra to be one of the most isolated non-volcanic landforms on the planet, and its millions of years of isolation from other land masses is responsible for its famously biodiverse ecosystems.

Among them is the Detwah Lagoon on the island's northwest coast, a Ramsar wetland and the only place on Socotra where the

vulnerable leopard stingray and the near threatened bluespotted ribbontail ray have been recorded. Forming a snow-white arc around this turquoise tidal inlet directly north of Qalansiyah town is Qalansiyah Beach, Socotra's most spectacular stretch of sand. Backed by wind-sculpted dunes and 1312ft-high (400m) sandstone and granite cliffs, this dramatic coastal landscape is also an important roosting and feeding area for waterbirds, including the endangered Egyptian vulture and the vulnerable Socotra cormorant. Swim, snorkel and hike along the cliffs for magnificent beach and lagoon views.

GETTING THERE

A safer and typically cheaper alternative to flying via mainland Yemen, there are weekly direct flights from Abu Dhabi to peaceful Socotra. Visas can be arranged in advance via local tour operators.

Europe

LEFT Surfers wait for waves in the waters of Famara, Spain.

ABOVE The surreal volcanic landscape folds into the deep-turquoise glow of the Aegean at Sarakiniko, Greece.

Zlatni Rat Beach

BOL, BRAČ
CROATIA

SHAPED LIKE AN ARROW, this natural shape-shifting Blue Flag spit – whose name translates as 'Golden Horn' – juts out into the Adriatic from the south coast of the knockout-pretty Dalmatian island of Brač. The famous silver-and-alabaster pebble beach is backed by a swirl of bottle-green pine trees, all offset by the sparkling teal and indigo hues of the waves washing over the shore. As one of Croatia's most-hyped beaches, it can get busy (especially during the summer), so it's worth arriving early to laze under the pines in relative peace before the crowds trickle in and the winds pick up. Water sports abound, from kitesurfing to kayaking, and windsurfing is a big speciality, with peak conditions in late May/early June and late July/early August. Each side of the peninsula has around 1640ft (500m) of beach, but the outline changes all the time with the coastal currents, and the promontory is growing every year thanks to the forces of Mother Nature. In the northwest corner there's a sheltered naturist area.

GETTING THERE
The loveliest way to reach Zlatni Rat is along the shaded 1.2-mile (2km) coastal promenade from Bol's mellow old town, though there are also short-hop boat services. Bol is 28 miles (45km) southeast of Supetar, on Brač's southern coast. The island is linked to Split (home to an international airport) by regular ferry (one hour).

Punta Rata Beach

BRELA, MAKARSKA RIVIERA
CROATIA

A MESMERISING ELECTRIC-GREEN SWEEP of dense Aleppo pine forests trickling down to meet the wonderfully clear Adriatic Sea sets the scene for one of the Croatian coast's most exquisite beaches. On the 37-mile (60km) Makarska Riviera, a short journey southeast of Split along the Dalmatian coast, the entire littoral around the low-key beach town of Brela feels like a feast of glowing white-pebble coves. But the dreamiest of all is Punta Rata, which extends 1312ft (400m) or so around a sublime headland protected by a nature reserve for decades. The

GETTING THERE

The beach is on the northwest edge of Brela (easily reached by walking or cycling), around 31 miles (50km) southeast of Split on Croatia's Dalmatian coast. Split has an international airport and good bus links to Brela (one hour).

fragrant pine groves provide plenty of shade, and paddling in the deep aqua water here is bliss, with temperatures well into the 70s (°F)/20s (°C) from June to October. Head out snorkelling, kayaking or stand-up paddleboarding, then stay on to catch a jaw-droppingly beautiful sunset over the much-photographed pine-dotted outcrop that rises from the sea. A view-heavy seafront promenade curves along the coast from Brela's harbour, passing a couple of other tempting coves along the way.

Rhossili Bay

GOWER
WALES

FAMOUSLY A FAVOURITE COASTAL ESCAPE of the early-
20th-century Welsh poet Dylan Thomas, Rhossili dazzles with its almost three miles
(5km) of honey-toned, Atlantic-beaten sands. Part of the 73-sq-mile (188-sq-km)
Gower Area of Outstanding Natural Beauty, this wonderfully secluded pocket of
Wales retains a special soul-stirring energy, framed by blonde dunes and Rhossili
Down's heather-scented slopes. For many, this is also one of the UK's finest surf
beaches and the vibrant scene buzzes year-round, with experienced surfers flocking
to Rhossili's north end and beginners finding their feet along its southern stretch.
But there's so much space to spread out that things never feel crowded. Keep an eye
out for choughs, kestrels, buntings and other feathered species soaring high above.
Seals and dolphins are sometimes spotted here too, and there are wonderful walking
routes along the Wales Coast Path. At low tide you can walk out to Worm's Head
(careful with the currents), a tidal island with terrific views across the beach cradled
beneath a bowl of cliffs from where paragliders set off.

GETTING THERE
Rhossili Bay sits at the westernmost end of Wales' Gower
peninsula, 19 miles (30km) west
of Swansea. Local buses run
between Swansea and Rhossili
village (one hour), from where
a steep path leads down to the
beach.

© Leighton Collins / Shutterstock

Rauðasandur

WESTFJORDS
ICELAND

ICELAND'S WILDLY BEAUTIFUL natural landscapes fire the imagination, and the spectacular yet still little-touristed Westfjords region in the northwest of the country tops the wow-factor list. It's here, among the plunging sea cliffs of this remote mountainous peninsula's southern coast, that you'll discover distant Rauðasandur – a 6-mile-long (10km) surf-washed beauty with a glinting turquoise lagoon, snaking through an endless sprawl of sand tinged in hues of red, orange and pink. A bumpy, twisting gravel road sets the scene, before you emerge on a deep bay cradled between steeply cascading bluffs (visit at low tide to stroll out along the sand). Considering most of Iceland's beaches are volcanic black-sand strands, this is an instantly special place. All those magical colours come from pulverised scallop shells and there's often not a single other person in sight. Grey and harbour seals are sometimes spotted frolicking around the shoreline here too. The surrounding area has some superb hiking trails, and it's possible to walk all the way between Rauðasandur and the famous Látrabjarg bird cliffs on the country's westernmost tip, where millions of puffins, razorbills, gannets, terns and other feathered species gather during warmer months.

GETTING THERE

Rauðasandur sits 19 miles (30km) south of Patreksfjörður in the Westfjords, which can be reached by one-hour flight from Reykjavík, by driving (it's around 640 miles/400km from Reykjavík to Patreksfjörður) or by catching the Baldur car ferry from Stykkishólmur (106 miles/170km north of Reykjavík). The Westfjords' often-unpaved roads require time, patience, advance planning and a sturdy, ideally 4WD vehicle.

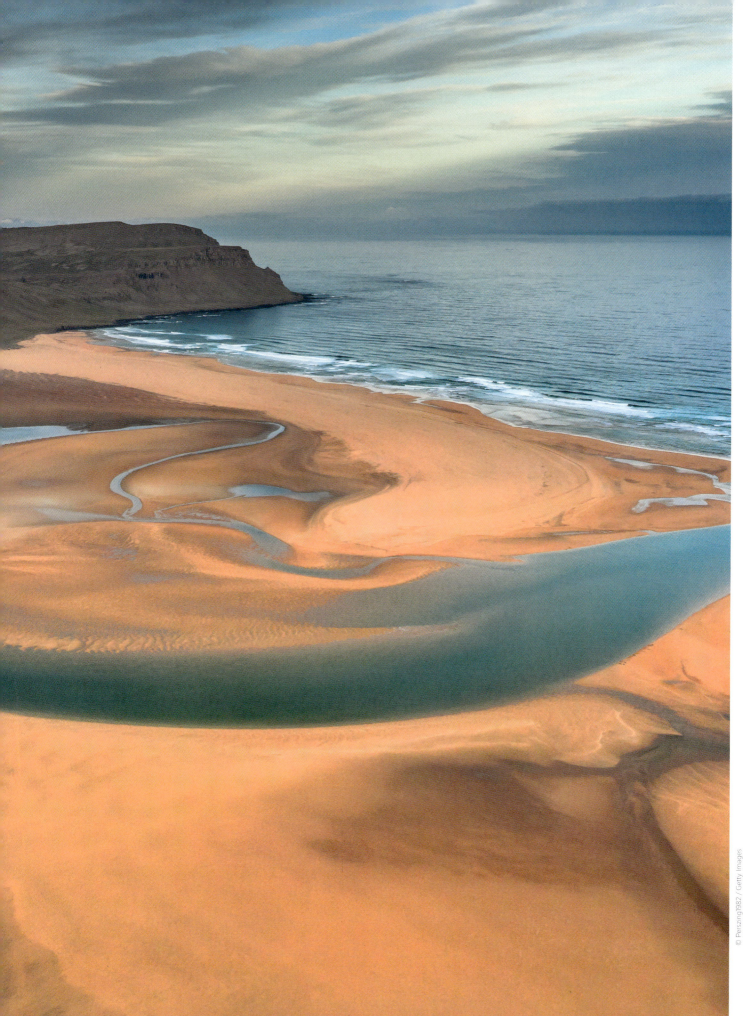

Calanque d'En-Vau

CASSIS, PROVENCE
FRANCE

PLUNGING COASTAL CLIFFS, scented pine forests, outstanding hiking, glorious back-to-nature coves – the 199-sq-mile (515-sq-km) Parc National des Calanques is a slice of Mediterranean heaven on Marseille's doorstep. The most soul-stirring of three protected and isolated *calanques* (coves) hidden just west of Cassis, En-Vau sits deep within a cliff-edged inlet and requires an on-foot adventure to reach. Drink in the beautiful scenery as you follow a steep, challenging footpath past the neighbouring beaches of Port-Miou and Port-Pin to finally reach this delectable cove, keeping your eyes peeled for Bonelli's eagles and other birds along the way. Slipping into the calm turquoise and sapphire water beneath the limestone cliffs and relaxing on the small, pale-shingle beach (all completely inaccessible by road) is the immense reward. The magnificent seaside crags here are a magnet for climbers, and wild boar are sometimes spotted in the area.

GETTING THERE
The remote cove is three miles (5km) southwest of Cassis and 12 miles (20km) southeast from Marseille. To get here, follow the 2.4-mile (3.8km) hiking trail from Calanque de Port-Miou (around 1½ hours), which is on the western edge of Cassis and reachable by car. Or you could head over by boat or kayak from Cassis.

Plage des Poulains

BELLE-ÎLE-EN-MER, BRITTANY
FRANCE

BRITTANY'S CRAGGY COAST reaches a spectacular crescendo at 12-mile-long (20km) Belle-Île-en-Mer, just off the Quiberon peninsula. Some of northern France's finest wild beaches lie tucked away among the island's 50-plus strands – many of them can only be reached on foot. At the far northwest end of Belle-Île, a small, dusty-blonde cove hugs the windswept Pointe des Poulains promontory, spilling over into a sandbar that often disappears at high tide. Bathed by the cool Atlantic and framed by low rocky cliffs, Plage des Poulains is at its calmest in July/August, when water temperatures peak at around 68°F (20°C) (take care with currents). Sunsets here are a treat, and it's easy to see why French actress Sarah Bernhardt spent almost every summer at Pointe des Poulains. In spring, bright-yellow gorse flowers burst into bloom along the shoreline. A rewarding way to arrive is by hiking along part of the 53-mile (85km) coastal path that loops around the entire island, linking Plage des Poulains with the pretty fishing village of Sauzon via a clutch of other tempting coves (around 3.7 miles/6km each way).

GETTING THERE
Pointe des Poulains is on the northwest tip of Belle-Île-en-Mer, which sits 10.5 miles (17km) off the French mainland in southern Brittany. There are year-round ferries to/from Quiberon (50 minutes). From spring to autumn, ferries also run between the island and other mainland destinations such as Vannes (two hours).

Plage de Palombaggia

PORTO-VECCHIO, CORSICA
FRANCE

ULTRA-CLEAR PALE TURQUOISE WATER ripples onto gold-white sand; pine trees stretch behind a slender 1.2-mile-long (2km) bay; and the bird-rich Îles Cerbicale (a protected nature reserve) glint on the horizon. Wedged into the southeast coast of the island just outside stylish Porto-Vecchio, Palombaggia is Corsica's most heavenly beach, and one of its most popular. Though there are a few waterside restaurants and sunbeds and umbrellas to rent, it's still a beautifully undeveloped place where you can

just laze on the flour-soft sand and go snorkelling around the orange-pink rocks towards either end of the beach. September and October are lovely months for swimming, with the calm translucent water at around 68 to 77°F (20 to 25°C) if you're braving the summer crowds, head over early. Sunset is a rewarding time to be here too, watching the day's final rays casting their warm glow across the art-worthy beachscape.

GETTING THERE

Palombaggia lies six miles (10km) southeast of Porto-Vecchio in southern Corsica – around a 20-minute drive. In July and August there's a shuttle bus to/from Porto-Vecchio. Corsica's four international airports mean handy links with destinations across Europe, and it's also easy to reach the island by ferry.

Playa de Torimbia

LLANES, ASTURIAS
SPAIN

～～～

PLENTY OF SPANIARDS WILL TELL YOU that some of their country's most divine beaches are hidden away along the wild, less-touristed northern coast, particularly in the lusciously green, cider-producing Asturias region. Between two rocky headlands, just outside Llanes (a lively fishing town), rippling green fields cascade down to a gold-sand conch-shaped bay washed by the moody-blue Bay of Biscay. This is serene Torimbia, one of Asturias' most-loved beaches and one of Spain's original naturist spots since the 1960s, thanks to its secluded natural setting. Though the sea here is often cooler than on Spain's Mediterranean coastline, in summer months temperatures easily rise to over 68°F (20°C). The final mile down to the sand from the *mirador* (lookout) high above involves a walk along a dirt track, so there's usually a pretty peaceful scene. Apart from a summer-only *chiringuito* (beach restaurant), you'll need to bring all your own snacks, drinks and beach gear. In spring gorgeous wildflowers burst into bloom across the surrounding hills. Torimbia's sister cove Toranda, just east, is another northern beauty worth seeking out.

～～～

GETTING THERE
Torimbia lies 5½ miles (9km) west of Llanes on the eastern Asturias coast, just beyond Niembro village. There's no public transport, so people tend to drive to the parking area then walk down, or hike along the coast to reach Torimbia. The nearest airports are Asturias (near Oviedo and Gijón) and Santander. It's also possible to reach Asturias by train from elsewhere in Spain (including Madrid), or by international ferry.

Platja Illetes

FORMENTERA, BALEARIC ISLANDS
SPAIN

FROM THE CLEAR CARIBBEAN-BLUE waters to
the carefree Mediterranean-island vibe, there's nowhere quite
like barefoot, salty-aired Formentera. The smallest of Spain's four
Balearics sits just southeast of Ibiza, and gorgeous Platja Illetes
evokes all that's magical about this beach paradise with a strong
sustainable vision. The beach sits on the west side of northern
Formentera's sand-dusted Trucador Peninsula, where a handful of
chiringuitos (beach restaurants) keep busy and flamingos wander
through shimmering lagoons. It's all part of the Unesco-listed,

65-sq-mile (168-sq-km) Parc Natural de Ses Salines, which protects the sprawling underwater posidonia seagrass meadows that make Formentera's waters so beautifully translucent. Days melt away between lazing on the silken sand, swimming in the gentle waves that fold from aquamarine to cobalt and feasting on rice dishes overlooking the water. Just beyond Illetes off the peninsula's northern tip lies uninhabited S'Espalmador islet – another white-sand knockout separated by a submerged sandbar.

GETTING THERE

During summer months, fast regular boats hop across to Platja Illetes from Formentera's La Savina port, continuing to S'Espalmador, and there are buses to from La Savina too. You can also day trip by boat from Ibiza, though we recommend lingering. There's no airport in Formentera, so the best way to get here is to catch a flight or a ferry to Ibiza Town, then an onward ferry (30 minutes to an hour).

Playa de Famara

LANZAROTE, CANARY ISLANDS
SPAIN

~~~

CURLED INTO LAID-BACK Lanzarote's untamed north coast, around 620 miles (1000km) southwest of the Spanish mainland, Famara ranks among Europe's greatest surf beaches. Strong Atlantic swells pull in wave-riders from all over the continent and beyond, and even just whispering the name 'Famara' guarantees a blissful in-the-know smile among the many fans of this all-natural Canarian haven. Like so many other beaches in Spain's Canary Islands, the spectacularly wild space has been shaped by a long volcanic history – a golden three-mile (5km) stretch of coast disappears into the distance beneath the lava-moulded crags of the Risco de Famara cliffs, which tower over 2000ft (650m) tall. Overlooking it all, tiny La Caleta de Famara village blends lively surf schools and cool cafes with traditional seafood restaurants and whitewashed Lanzarote-style houses. Each evening, people gather on Famara's sands as the sun blazes orangey pink over neighbouring Isla Graciosa. Have a go with a surfing class, try some beach yoga or simply drink in the view from a perch among the rolling dunes.

GETTING THERE

Famara is 12 miles (20km) north of Lanzarote's capital Arrecife, easily reached by local bus (35 minutes), by driving (25 minutes) or even cycling. Lanzarote has international flights to/from destinations all over Europe, as well as ferry links with the neighbouring islands of Fuerteventura and Gran Canaria and (less frequent) the mainland Spanish cities of Cádiz and Huelva.

Cala Estreta

COSTA BRAVA, CATALONIA
SPAIN

SUNRISE CASTS A HAZY GLOW across a sparkling half-moon *cala* (cove) at one of the most seductive little beaches hidden away along Catalonia's pretty Costa Brava, which stretches northeast from Barcelona all the way to the French border. With scented pine forests and dusty walking paths trickling down to a pebble-and-sand strand where the Mediterranean melts into a million blues, Cala Estreta is a classic Costa Brava scene. Set within the Espai Natural Castell-Cap Roig (a local nature reserve), the clothing-optional beach is only accessible on foot and has a curious, centuries-old fishing hut huddled by the shore. Plunge into the sea here before hiking back to Calella for a platter of the freshest locally sourced seafood or a perfectly cooked *fideuà* (paella-style noodle dish) overlooking the waves. Or bring supplies for the day and settle in to soak up the views across the craggy Formigues islets just offshore.

GETTING THERE

The most rewarding way to reach Cala Estreta is by hiking along the coastal paths from Calella, Platja de Castell or further afield; many of the area's walking routes follow the long-distance GR92 or the ancient *camins de ronda* trails. There are local buses from Palafrugell to Calella (30 minutes), and you can easily reach Palafrugell by bus from Girona (one hour) or Barcelona (2¼ hours).

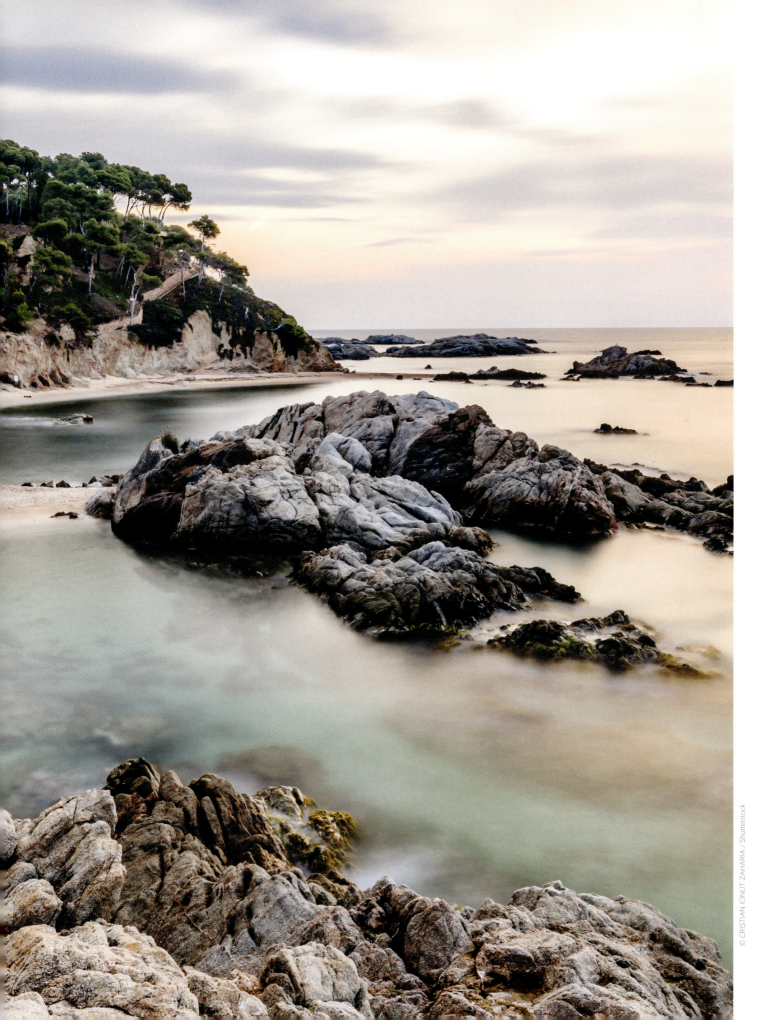

Punta Paloma

TARIFA, CÁDIZ
SPAIN

SAY *HOLA* TO THE SULTRY Andalucian beach paradise you've been dreaming of. On mainland Europe's southernmost tip, the blissfully undeveloped beaches around the kitesurf-loving town of Tarifa are some of Spain's most spectacular, and dune-blessed Punta Paloma might just be the most seductive of them all.

Choosing a favourite Spanish beach feels almost impossible, but the moment you glimpse Punta Paloma's satin-soft sands and dunes set against a backdrop of Morocco and the wind-lashed Strait of Gibraltar, it's obvious why playa-loving Spaniards rave about Cádiz' bewitching Costa de la Luz. Sparkling under the crisp southern sun, this pale-blonde boho-feeling beauty wows everyone from first-timers to long-time local residents. Colourful kites whizz across the horizon, swimmers plunge into the cobalt Atlantic waves, and blissed-out beachgoers sip cool *tinto con limón* (red wine with lemonade) at the sand-hugging *chiringuito* (beach restaurant).

Clamber up the shifting dunes at sunset for a dazzling view of Tarifa's shoreline backed by Morocco's Rif Mountains and over the perfumed pine forests that stretch into the distance behind Punta Paloma. Stroll along the sand to the west end of the curving beach, where you can lather on a mineral-rich natural mud bath. Or hike north along the coast to dream-like Bolonia, where another white-sand wonder awaits in the shadow of a major ruined Roman town, Baelo Claudia. Rewarding walking and horse-riding routes weave into the rugged surrounding hills too, including curious sights such as the prehistoric Los Algarbes necropolis.

Much of Cádiz' Costa de la Luz – whose sublime sugar-white sands roll more than 125 miles (200km) between Sanlúcar de

Barrameda and Tarifa – is protected in one shape or another, which has kept tourism development to a minimum for its lovely whitewashed villages. Punta Paloma sits within the 74-sq-mile (192-sq-km) Parque Natural del Estrecho, a wild reserve known for its flocks of migratory birds flying between Europe and Africa and for the many dolphins, turtles and whales that patrol its Atlantic waters (whale-watching excursions head out across the Strait from spring to autumn). Things still get busy in July and August, but centuries-old Tarifa town remains an easy-breezy beauty with sloping cobbled streets, inspiring international-influenced restaurants, a smattering of creative boutique hotels and a unique salt-in-the-air allure.

It's all down to the always-buzzing surf scene, fired by the famous *levante* wind. Kitesurfing might be all the rage these days, but the North African-feeling town was first put on the international wave-riding map when windsurfers arrived in the 1980s. Now an ever-growing wave of schools offers everything from beginner courses to advanced training. Much of the fun happens on Tarifa's cream-sand Valdevaqueros beach, but you'll spot all the action from neighbouring Punta Paloma while also sidestepping the high-summer crowds. If you're keen to learn the ropes, May/June and September are the best months to start out.

GETTING THERE

Punta Paloma is 6.2 miles (10km) northwest of Tarifa and linked by bus during summer months only. Tarifa is easily reached by car or bus from Málaga, Gibraltar, Jerez or Seville, all of which have international airports.

Sylt

NORTH FRISIAN ISLANDS
GERMANY

ALONG THE WINDSWEPT COAST of Germany's northernmost island, just west of the mainland near the Danish border, thousands of nautical-striped cocoon-like Strandkorb beach sofas dot a stunningly elemental coastal landscape. The largest of the North Frisian Islands, low-rise Sylt has long been a hub for chic beach holidays thanks to its 25-mile (40km) coastline blessed with wide-open, dune-dusted sands trickling into the North Sea. The entire west coast is one never-ending sprawl of shimmering, untouched alabaster sand disappearing into the distant haze, with the odd beachfront sauna and some great surf thrown into the mix. Between celebrity haven Kampen and family-friendly Wenningstedt, ochre-tinged sandstone cliffs back the beach for several kilometres and boardwalks weave through the dunes – this is a particularly special space when bathed in a warm sunset glow. Typical water temperatures wander from around 54°F (12°C) in early May to 72°F (22°C) in August, though do take care with currents. Back in 1920, Sylt became the first place in Germany to welcome an official naturist beach, and there are still plenty of spots for anyone who fancies a swimsuit-free day by the sea.

GETTING THERE
Sylt's small airport has seasonal flights to and from destinations across Germany. Otherwise, the best way to arrive is by rail from the mainland town of Niebüll (35 minutes). Sylt's train station is at the main town of Westerland, and trains can also transport cars. Once here, hop on a bike to explore or make use of local buses and well-signed walking routes. It's also possible to get to Sylt by ferry from Denmark's Rømø island.

Paralia Tis Grias to Pidima

ANDROS, CYCLADES
GREECE

A ROCKY OUTCROP soaring 69ft (21m) out of the glittering aquamarine Aegean makes this small, silvery-gold strand in southeast Andros one of the dreamiest back-to-nature beaches in the Cyclades. Entirely free from sun loungers, umbrellas and restaurants, it has a mellow feel, with craggy cliffs framing the powdery sand around one mile (1.6km) north of Ormos. According to legend, an elderly woman jumped off the towering sea crag and miraculously turned to stone, giving the beach its

curious name – 'The Old Woman's Leap'. Hiking over from nearby Korthi harbour is part of the fun; approaching along the dusty unpaved track, you'll spot a whitewashed chapel resting atop the cliffs. Pack a picnic, a swimsuit, a book and a sunhat – the water here is particularly delicious for swimming from July to September, when temperatures hover around 77°F (25°C). Further afield, the whole island is a haven for hikers; don't miss the rewarding trails weaving through the lush, waterfall-laced interior.

GETTING THERE

The beach is 16 miles (25km) south of Andros' elegant main town, Hora. If driving, you'll follow a dirt track before walking the last half-mile (0.8km) or so down. Andros has regular ferry links with Athens' Rafina port (one to two hours), as well as other Greek islands such as Mykonos (1¼ to 2¼ hours) and Tinos (one to two hours); flying into Mykonos International Airport then catching the ferry to Andros is a convenient option.

Kokkinokastro

ALONNISOS, SPORADES

GREECE

FLUNG OUT IN THE NORTHERN Aegean Sea, around 31 miles (50km) north of Evia, lush Alonnisos remains the least-touristed of the four magical main Sporades Islands. Fragrant with herbs, pines and fruit orchards, this easy-going island sits within the 1004-sq-mile (2260-sq-km) National Marine Park of Alonnisos Northern Sporades, which means the water washing onto its unspoilt beaches is glassily clear.

Among the most spectacular of mountainous Alonnisos' many sultry beaches is Kokkinokastro – an east-coast jewel whose name translates as 'Red Castle', 4 miles (6km) northeast of Patitiri port. A craggy rust-red cape juts out into the unbelievably blue water, while a silvery pebble-and-sand curve curls into the bay below backed by bottle-green pine trees. With a seasonal beach bar, a refreshingly wild feel and just a few sunbeds to rent, this is a divine spot to simply kick back with a good book, dip into the gentle turquoise waves and drink in the views of the uninhabited offshore islets. But there's intriguing history to uncover here too: the ruined wall of ancient Ikos city (now underwater) is still visible if you look closely, and a collection of Paleolithic tools was also found in the area.

Kokkinokastro and its sister beaches owe much of their pristine beauty to the surrounding national marine park. Declared back in 1992, it protects the endangered Mediterranean monk seal, as well as swathes of oxygen-producing posidonia seagrass. You'd be lucky to spot a Mediterranean monk seal, though there's always a chance – as of 2023, only 800 or so of these famously reclusive creatures remain (half of them in Greece), with pups usually born

in dimly lit caves far away from any potential danger. Other local residents include rare seabirds such as Eleonora's falcons, various turtle and dolphin species, and whales passing through as they migrate across the Mediterranean. There are wonderful boat trips out into the marine park from Alonnisos during summer months, on which you might spot one of these animals and you can also visit remote Kyra Panagia island with its 1200 CE-founded monastery.

For the full island wow-factor, stay in evocative Old Alonnisos, where you can admire the dreamy shoreline from a 656ft-high (200m) hilltop perch.

GETTING THERE

Easily accessible by driving from anywhere on the island, Kokkinokastro sits halfway between Patitiri (Alonnisos's main port) and Steni Vala village on the east coast. Alonnisos has year-round ferry links with Agios Constantinos (four hours) and Volos (three hours) on the Greek mainland, via Skiathos and Skopelos; first you'll need to catch a bus from Athens to Agios Constantinos or Volos. It's also possible to fly into Skiathos then catch the ferry onwards to Alonnisos (two hours); international flights to/from Skiathos mostly only operate seasonally (May to September), but there are year-round flights between Athens and Skiathos.

Elafonisi

HANIA, CRETE
GREECE

THE GLINT OF GENTLE emerald waves rolling onto soft dusty-pink sand creates a fairy-tale scene at mesmerising Elafonisi, pocketed away on the southwest tip of sun-toasted Crete. All those shimmering rosy hues come from shells ground down over millennia. The main beach swirls around lagoon-like shallow water, making it perfect for cooling off and for kids to splash around, while sunbeds dot the shoreline under straw-topped umbrellas. At certain times of day, a slender sandbar links the beach with dune-filled

Elafonisi Islet, just 490ft (150m) offshore, which is favoured by naturists and has dazzling views, as well as a cluster of small, quieter coves. To help protect this fragile yet hugely popular natural space from overtourism, we recommend dropping by in shoulder season (May/June, September/October) or even the winter months (November to March) – there might be few facilities and little public transport then, but you'll get to savour Elafonisi's immense beauty more peacefully.

© Patryk Kosmider / Shutterstock

GETTING THERE
Elafonisi lies 43 miles (70km) southwest from the history-rich town of Hania (around a 1½-hour drive), and you can easily wade across to the islet from the main beach. From June to September there are also boat and boat services from nearby Paleohora (one hour) and buses from Hania (2¼ hours). Hania's airport has year-round domestic flights, as well as seasonal international routes.

Myrtos Beach

KEFALLONIA, IONIANS
GREECE

RESTING AT THE FOOT of a dramatically zigzagging road in northern Kefallonia, off the western Greek mainland, Myrtos remains one of the most-photographed and entrancing beaches in a country bursting with glorious Mediterranean-lapped sands. Spin past the twirling vines, hot-pink oleanders, lushly forested head-lands and sheer marble-hued cliffs of the largest Ionian island. At the road's base you'll reach this sprawling Blue Flag-awarded expanse of bone-white pebbles and irresistible water that shifts like a dream from turquoise to sky-blue to deep sapphire. Sure, it's a popular place, but jumping right into those glinting blue waves or even just glimpsing the view from up high instantly soothes the soul. And as the sun begins to sink each evening, pinks and oranges bounce off the limestone-clad landscape. May to October is the best swimming season. If you're visiting during summer, head over first thing to beat the crowds and bag a prized parking spot or a sun lounger under the straw-topped umbrellas.

GETTING THERE
Myrtos is 15.5 miles (25km) north of Kefallonia's 'capital' Argostoli, near Divarata village – around a 45-minute drive. Buses run between Argostoli and Myrtos during the summer season; it's best to check the latest schedules locally. Kefallonia has flights to and from international and Greek destinations, and is also well-connected by ferry, including with Lefkada (one to two hours), Zakynthos (three hours) and the Peloponnese Peninsula (many routes are seasonal).

Sarakiniko

MILOS, CYCLADES
GREECE

ALONG THE NORTHERN SHORELINE of heavenly Milos, at the southwestern point of Greece's Cyclades Islands, a surreal volcanic landscape folds into the deep-turquoise glow of the Aegean. Welcome to Sarakiniko, where there's just a tiny stretch of sand and you'll need to bring all your own supplies. A swirl of bare, velvety silver-white rocks rolls along the water, sculpted over the centuries by wave-and-wind erosion and various eruptions. Stone arches, alabaster cliffs, disused mining tunnels and dimly lit caves create a mesmerising contrast with the endless sea blues. Swimmers and snorkellers slip straight off the rocks into a meandering inlet; others plunge in from the cliffs high above the glinting water. On an island home to over 70 beaches (more than any other in the Cyclades), it's no surprise that this otherworldly spot ranks among the country's most-loved beaches. Swing by outside high season to sidestep the crowds (September and October are usually a joy), or visit first thing to soak up the salty early-morning breeze with plenty of space to spread out. At sunset, Sarakiniko's lunar-like rock formations take on a whole new magic.

GETTING THERE

Sarakiniko is 1.9 miles (3km) north of Adamas port, on Milos' northern-most coast. Several daily buses run here from Adamas during summer months and there's parking for anyone arriving by scooter, car or ATV. Milos airport has domestic flights to and from Athens, or you can also reach Milos by ferry from Athens' Piraeus port (2½ to 6½ hours) as well as other islands such as Santorini (two hours).

Baia di Ieranto

NERANO, AMALFI COAST
ITALY

A KNOCKOUT BACK-TO-NATURE pebble beach gazing out on Capri's famed Isole Faraglioni, Ieranto lures hikers to the blissfully undeveloped tip of the Sorrento peninsula. The whole place is part of the Amalfi Coast's Punta Campanella Marine Reserve and is also protected by the environment-focused Fondo Ambiente Italiano organisation, which means no development or motor vehicles are permitted. The only way to get here is by following a rocky 1.2-mile (2km) walking trail from the square in the village of Nerano, which takes around 45 minutes and has some steep sections. Once you arrive, the reward is a mesmerising, classic Amalfi scene of plunging sea cliffs, fragrant olive trees and electric-blue water. Both sheltered and secluded, this is a dreamy place for swimming and snorkelling in the deliciously translucent Mediterranean. In Greek mythology, it was here that Odysseus met the sirens on his journey home to Ithaca. Bring sturdy footwear, plenty of water and some snacks; if you're swinging by in summer, head out early to beat the heat and the crowds.

GETTING THERE
Baia di Ieranto is around nine miles (15km) southwest of Sorrento, accessible only on foot from Nerano village (around a 45-minute walk). Nerano has a few daily bus links to/from nearby Sorrento (50 minutes).

Cala Goloritzé

GOLFO DI OROSEI, SARDINIA
ITALY

With the Tyrrhenian Sea's emerald waters reflecting like glass off the wild limestone sea cliffs, eastern Sardinia's Golfo di Orosei hosts some of the most wondrous beaches in the entire Mediterranean. Towards the southern end of this paradise-like gulf, a small stretch of powdery sugar-white pebble beach sits cradled beneath soaring rock formations. The sea gleams in teal and indigo, and the jagged coastline looms into view all around. Getting to secluded Cala Goloritzé is half the adventure, involving a steep 2.2-mile (3.5km) trail down from the Altopiano del Golgo near Baunei, around an hour's walk. It's worth every second once you slip into the crystalline water, or dive in with a snorkel. Rock climbers are tempted here by the 486ft-high (148m) Monte Caroddi (also known as Aguglia) formation, a natural stone spire soaring above the bay. The cove (and much of the surrounding coastal landscape) is protected by Sardinia's major national park, the 286-sq-mile (740-sq-km) Parco Nazionale del Golfo di Orosei e del Gennargentu. To help preserve the fragile natural environment, there are no beach services and at the time of writing a cap of 250 visitors a day had been introduced (with a small entrance fee and prebooking required).

GETTING THERE
Cala Goloritzé is 100 miles (160km) northeast of Cagliari, near Baunei village in eastern Sardinia. It's around the same distance from the Costa Smeralda's Olbia Airport in northern Sardinia. If you aren't hiking in along the trail, it's possible to reach the beach by boat, but it's best to check the latest access regulations in advance.

© maniscule / Getty Images

Cala Capreria

RISERVA NATURALE DELLO ZINGARO, SICILY
ITALY

~~~~~~~~

SEDUCTIVE SICILY'S 930-mile (1500km) coast bursts with swoon-worthy sand and swim spots, but peak months can draw serious crowds to the island's most-celebrated beaches. Hidden away along the Golfo di Castellammare on the northwest coast, the blissful Riserva Naturale dello Zingaro is a feast of small, peaceful pebble calette (coves) encircled by rust-tinged cliffs and bathed by the bright-turquoise Tyrrhenian Sea. A 4.3-mile (7km) coastal path threads through the park's seven tempting Mediterranean-vibe beaches, which include tiny Cala Capreria near the southern entrance. Stairs lead down to a curl of silvery pebbles, where cooling off with a swim surrounded by craggy cliffs is a treat. Bring snacks, water and an umbrella for shade, as there are no facilities here. The entire 6-sq-mile (16-sq-km) nature reserve is a haven for hikers, who might spot Bonelli's eagles and other birds soaring high above the trails that weave among the wild thyme, almond trees and Aleppo pines.

~~~~~~~~

GETTING THERE
The main access point for the Riserva Naturale dello Zingaro is 1.2 miles (2km) north of Scopello, at the south end of the park. From here, it's about a mile (1.4km) north to Cala Capreria, which is linked to coves further north by a beautiful coastal path. Scopello is 47 miles (75km) west of Palermo, around a 1¼-hour drive.

Sveti Stefan Beach

BUDVA
MONTENEGRO

THE FORTIFIED, HONEY-WALLED 15th-century island village of Sveti Stefan (now a private luxury resort) makes up the spectacular backdrop to this Adriatic pearl. Just across the delicious blue-green sea from the islet, the unspoilt pebble-and-sand beach sweeps around a small, curving mainland bay. Towards the northwest end, it narrows to a wonderfully scenic double-beach isthmus, though the pay-to-use stretch on the north side is part of the resort. There's great swimming with the deep, translucent water hovering around the mid- to high 70s (°F)/20s (°C) from June to October, plus sunbeds to rent – or just pick your slice of Montene-grin paradise and spread out on the rocks. The coast around Budva (Montenegro's most ancient seaside city) dazzles with some of the most ravishing beaches in the Med, but few can rival Sveti Stefan's magical natural setting. No wonder glamorous icons Marilyn Mon-roe and Elizabeth Taylor both once spent time here.

GETTING THERE
Just outside Budva on Montenegro's central coast, Sveti Stefan sits 19 miles (30km) southeast of Tivat's international airport, which has plenty of seasonal routes and a few year-round flights. Budva is well-linked by bus, including to Dubrovnik in Croatia (three hours).

© instacruising / Shutterstock

Haukland Beach

VESTVÅGØY, LOFOTEN ISLANDS
NORWAY

GAWPING AT THE NORTHERN LIGHTS reflecting off snow-white sands feels like pure magic on northern Norway's remote Lofoten archipelago, where Haukland Beach rests against a majestic mountain backdrop on western Vestvågøy. Set between bright-green hills, Haukland has a blinding stretch of luscious sand bathed by cool Arctic waters. The sea doesn't really creep higher than around 59°F (15°C) (and that's in August), but the spectacular natural setting still makes this one of the most unbelievably beautiful spots among Norway's thousands of beaches. Or grab a wetsuit and join anyone else braving the waters here. There's plenty of kayaking and stand-up paddleboarding for enjoying the scenery from out on the water, not to mention terrific hiking and the chance to camp overlooking the beach. Trails lead up the mountains encircling the bay, opening up sprawling views, as well as to neighbouring Uttakleiv Beach (another jewel). When summer swings around, the midnight sun bathes the whole place in an eerie glow.

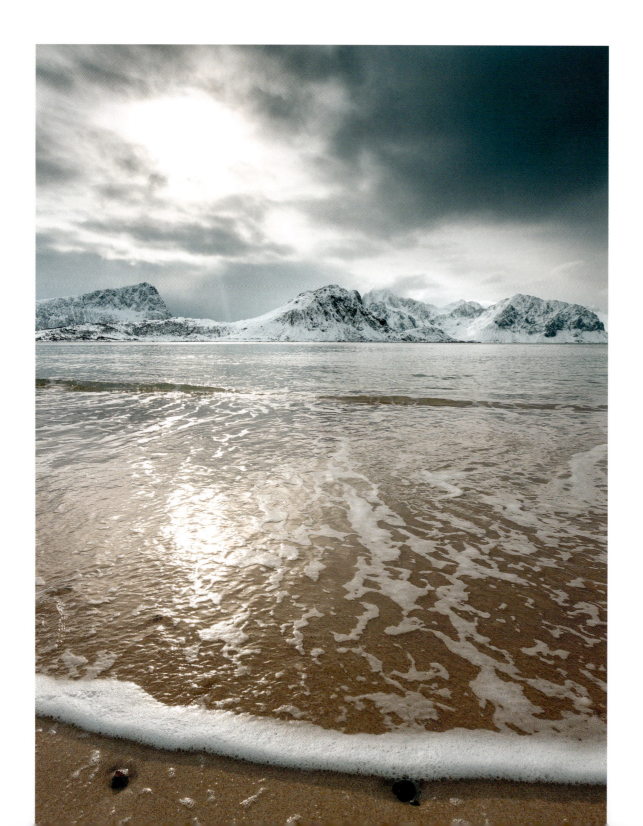

GETTING THERE

Haukland is on the west coast of Vestvågøy, Lofoten's second-major
island, and is easily reached by car or bus from nearby Leknes, which is
six miles (10km) south of the beach. Leknes' small regional airport has
domestic flights to and from Oslo, Bodø and Tromsø, or you can fly or
catch the train to Bodø, then take a three-hour ferry to Moskenes in the
Lofoten archipelago.

Durdle Door Beach

LULWORTH, DORSET
ENGLAND

ON SOUTHERN DORSET'S Unesco-protected Jurassic Coast, a colossal almost-golden limestone sea arch wows as one of the UK's most-photographed coastal formations. Sculpted by the sea and wind, Durdle Door soars 200ft (61m) tall above the English Channel. Having begun its long journey around 150 million years ago, it is expected to eventually collapse back into the sea, leaving behind a stack. Swimming off the shingle-and-sand beach beneath the green-clad cliffs, with turquoise water stretching into the distance, is a special moment. Over 140 steps lead down to the strand and there are no facilities, which means all beach gear must be carried along. Between mid-December and mid-January, the sunrise shines right through the Durdle Door arch for just a few minutes each day – a mystical work of natural art that draws droves of photographers and onlookers. A one-mile (1.6km) walk east along the fossil-rich cliffs, following the long-distance South West Coast Path, leads to spectacular Lulworth Cove.

GETTING THERE

Durdle Door is a 25-mile (40km) drive southwest of Bournemouth on
the Dorset coast. Outdoors lovers will enjoy walking here along the
view-laden Dorset stretch of the South West Coast Path.

Kynance Cove

LIZARD, CORNWALL

ENGLAND

WHETHER YOU'VE HIKED for miles along the long-distance South West Coast Path or just fancy a paddle in the tempting teal waters, Kynance Cove stops everyone in their tracks. Curled into the west side of southern Cornwall's wild Lizard peninsula, near the southernmost tip of mainland England, this is one of the country's dreamiest beaches – a pristine all-natural inlet dominated by craggy serpentine-rock outcrops, stone-carved arches and grassy green headlands. It's best to visit at low tide, as much of the gorgeous silvery beach disappears into the water when the tide is up. But at any moment, taking in the astonishing scenery is a treat, ideally over a soul-warming coffee at the solar-powered seasonal cafe set in a reimagined fisher's cottage overlooking the bay. And on a sunny blue-sky day, Kynance easily rivals any beach in the Caribbean. Across the water, small tidal Asparagus Island gets its name from the rare wild asparagus that grows on its rocky cliffs.

GETTING THERE

Kynance Cove is 29 miles (47km) south of Truro (a one-hour drive) and 25 miles (40km) southeast of Penzance. The area is maintained by the UK's National Trust heritage conservation charity, which has a car park a 10-minute stroll from the beach. A wonderful way to reach the cove is by walking part of the South West Coast Path along Cornwall's dazzling shoreline.

Keem Bay Beach

KEEL, COUNTY MAYO
IRELAND

A VERTIGINOUS YET jaw-droppingly beautiful 4.9-mile (8km) drive from Keel village, at the distant western end of County Mayo's Achill Island, sets the scene for one of Ireland's most glorious, secluded strands. Sloping green hillsides spill down to a deep-set horseshoe bay, where a Blue-Flag delight of a pale-blonde beach sits framed by the Croaghaun Cliffs (Ireland's highest sea cliffs) and the thundering moody-blue Atlantic. The tucked away location means calm (if cool) waters, so swimming and snorkelling are popular. Summer kayaking trips are a fabulous way to drink

in the wild and rural scene from the water, and those with keen eyes might spot rare plankton-eating basking sharks and pods of dolphins, which sometimes swim and feed around the swirling bay. The famously scenic Wild Atlantic Way sweeps through Keem Bay on its 1600-mile-long (2600km) journey around the Irish coast. Don't miss the picturesque walk across the cliffs towards the westernmost tip of the island.

GETTING THERE
Keem Bay is accessible along western Achill Island's snaking R319 road. The nearest airport is Ireland West Airport Knock, 59 miles (95km) east of Achill Island, or a 1½-hour drive away, with some international flights.

Dueodde

NEXØ, BORNHOLM
DENMARK

A SECLUDED SWEEP OF GLISTENING, pearly-white sand dominates this protected natural space on the southern tip of Denmark's sunniest island, Bornholm, which lies closer to Sweden than the Danish mainland. Surrounded by the wild Baltic Sea, Bornholm is famous for its crisp natural light, as any visit to divine Dueodde reveals. Low waves tinged in shades of turquoise, jade and cerulean ripple along the dune-sprinkled shoreline, which curves for miles around the edge of the island. A series of trails and boardwalks leads through scented pine forests to the southernmost, widest stretch of sand, where the silky dunes double as protection from the wind. On a clear day, wading out across the shallow water almost feels like stepping into a painting. Sunsets here are magical, and the sprinkling of facilities are hidden well back from the sand (a campsite here, a cafe there). Cool winter months can bring snow to the beach – it's perfectly possible to see people tobogganing down the same sandbanks that simmered under the summer sun just a few months before. For wraparound coastal views, climb the 196 steps up Dueodde's blue-and-white 1960s lighthouse.

GETTING THERE

Dueodde's main patch of beach is 6.2 miles (10km) south of Nexø, at the southern end of Bornholm, around 125 miles (200km) east of Copenhagen. There are handy car parks at Fyrvejen and Skrokke-gards. Bornholm airport has year-round 35-minute flights to and from Copenhagen, as well as seasonal links with Berlin, Aarhus and more. There are also regular ferry services to and from Ystad in Sweden (1¼ hours).

© Sascha Steiner / Getty Images

Praia do Camilo

LAGOS, ALGARVE
PORTUGAL

BACKED BY SOARING Mesozoic limestone cliffs shaped by the elements over millennia, the golden beaches of the Algarve are as dramatic as they are lovely. Among the finest is Praia do Camilo, a small sandy cove on the outskirts of Lagos, a pretty resort town with cobbled lanes and picturesque squares enclosed by 16th-century walls.

Some 200 wooden steps help beachgoers descend to the small strip of sand that's lapped by shallow turquoise waters. Arrive early (or visit outside of the June to August peak season) to secure towel space. At the western end of the beach, a tunnel leads through the cliffs to teeny and similarly beautiful Praia do Boneca. Swim out from here on a calm day, and you'll find secluded rock pools and even tinier secret beaches that aren't accessible from the cliffs above. Enjoy another dazzling perspective on these idyllic beaches from the seat of a kayak or atop a stand-up paddleboard, both of which can be rented locally.

GETTING THERE
Praia do Camilo is 1.4 miles (2.2km) or a 25-minute walk from central Lagos. There's a small car park, and a restaurant, at the top of the cliffs.

West Beach

BERNERAY, OUTER HEBRIDES
SCOTLAND

THE POWDERY SILVER-WHITE SAND might feel more Southeast Asia than North Atlantic, but the chilly aqua waves, dramatic wind-lashed setting and beautifully green adjoining *machair* (grazing land) are pure, wonderful Outer Hebrides. This wildly remote jewel of a beach sprawls along almost three miles (5km) of untouched shoreline on tiny Berneray, off Scotland's northwest coast, where strolling beside the ocean and watching local wildlife are more the thing than swimming – the water here rarely rises over 55°F (13°C). A couple of isolated islets and the Harris Hills loom across the Sound of Harris, and the whole area is a paradise for bird-watchers, who might spot cormorants, gannets and more. In spring, the surrounding landscapes burst with wildflowers, and sea rocket grows on the beach during summer. Bring hiking shoes, layers and binoculars and brave the elements as you stroll through the grassy elevated dunes, perhaps continuing around the island's Atlantic-battered coast to smaller East Beach.

GETTING THERE
The beach stretches along the entire west coast of Berneray, which is linked by ferry to Leverburgh in neighbouring Harris (the southern half of the Outer Hebrides' main island). There are flights from Edinburgh, Inverness, Glasgow and Southampton to Stornoway Airport in Lewis (the northern half of the principal island), which also has ferry links. You'll want a car (or other wheels) to explore; it's worth booking ferry slots for vehicles in advance.

Kabak Beach

MUĞLA
TURKIYE

ONCE ONE OF TURKIYE'S MOST heavily guarded travel secrets, beautiful Kabak Beach is becoming better known these days, yet its out-of-the way location and lack of development (the construction of permanent buildings is not allowed in this protected valley) has helped Kabak to retain its castaway-esque magic. A lick of white sand surrounded by forested hills and lapped by the sapphire waters of the Mediterranean, Kabak is the kind of place you come to chill by the beach, and not much else. Though if you're feeling energetic, the famous Lycian Way – Turkiye's premier long-distance hiking trail – threads through Kabak. There's also a popular trail leading to a serene waterfall high up in the valley, with the option to take a heart-starting dip in the crystalline stream that flows from the bottom of the falls.

There are no roads in Kabak. From the bus stop, you'll need to descend the steep, rocky path to the beach, lined by simple accommodation with attached restaurants. There are a few small shops, but it's best to bring everything you will need for your stay.

GETTING THERE
Kabak Beach lies 20.5 miles (33km) or roughly an hour's drive south of Fethiye. From Fethiye's central bus station, hop on a minibus bound for Ölüdeniz, home to a beautiful beach of its own. Stay on the bus after it stops in Ölüdeniz until it reaches its last stop, Kabak, after around 30 minutes.

Americas

ABOVE   Surfers at sunset;
Cannon Beach, Oregon.
RIGHT   Bottom Bay, Barbados,
at sunset.

Ipanema Beach

RIO DE JANEIRO

BRAZIL

ONE LONG STRETCH of sun-drenched sand in Brazil's most famous coastal city, Ipanema Beach has been popular with sunseeking *cariocas* (residents of Rio de Janeiro) since 1902, when a new streetcar line made the beach on the southern fringe of the city easier to access. But it wasn't until 'The Girl From Ipanema' hit the airwaves in 1960s that the rest of the world caught on. The hit bossa nova and jazz song was reportedly inspired by a real-life local girl, Helô Pinheiro, that co-writers Antonio Carlos Jobim and Vinicius de Moraes saw walking past the Veloso bar (now the Garota de Ipanema, a block back from the beach) in the winter of 1962.

Ipanema Beach is itself an undeniable beauty, particularly when the sun sets behind the distinctive peaks of the Dois Irmãos (Two Brothers) to the west. Do as the locals do and clap as the sunset puts on its daily show.

Over 1.9 miles (3km) long, Ipanema Beach is demarcated by *postos* (posts, or in this case, numbered lifeguard towers), which mark off subcultures as diverse as the city itself. Posto 9, right off Rua Vinícius de Moraes, is where Rio's most lithe and tanned bodies migrate. The area is also known locally as Cemetério dos Elefantes because of the handful of old leftists, hippies and artists who sometimes hang out there. In front of Rua Farme de Amoedo is Praia Farme, the stomping ground for gay society.

Posto 8 further east is mostly the domain of favela kids. Arpoador (posto 7), between Ipanema and Copacabana, is Rio's most popular surf spot. Posto 10 is for sports lovers, where there are ongoing games of volleyball, soccer, *futevôlei* (footvolley) and *frescobol* (beach tennis played with wooden rackets and a rubber ball), while Leblon, west of Posto 10, attracts a broad mix of cariocas.

Whatever spot you choose, you'll enjoy cleaner sands and sea than those in neighbouring Copacabana, as well as people-watching galore as locals crowd in around you to sunbathe, picnic, play music and sports, and gossip. Go early on weekends to stake out a spot. Umbrellas and beach chairs can be rented from kiosks lining the beach, many of which also sell snacks and drinks – go on, order a caipirinha. Many of Ipanema's best restaurants are also just a short walk from the beach.

The word *ipanema* is an indigenous word for 'bad, dangerous waters', which is telling, given the strong undertow and often powerful waves that crash onto the shore. Take your cues from locals and swim where they do, in the safest spots.

Leaving valuables unattended on the beaches of Rio also isn't without risk; slip them into a waterproof bag that can be taken into the sea.

GETTING THERE

Ipanema Beach is in the South Zone of Rio de Janeiro. Av Vieira Souto runs alongside the beach.

Baía dos Porcos

FERNANDO DE NORONHA, PERNAMBUCO
BRAZIL

ONE OF THE SMALLEST BEACHES on the remote Fernando de Noronha archipelago, some 211 miles (340km) off Brazil's Atlantic coast, diminutive Baía dos Porcos is only accessible by foot. But this rocky cove on the Unesco-listed archipelago's eponymous main island, known simply as Noronha, is well worth the effort to reach.

A 98ft (30m) strip of golden sand lapped by azure waters and framed by volcanic rocks, the setting is simply sublime. Perch on the black rocks for sensational views of the Morros Dois Irmãos, or 'Two Brothers Hills' rising up out of the turquoise sea just off the beach. Paddle in the protected waters, and pack a picnic to enjoy on the sparkling sand. There are no pigs to be seen, but these highly protected islands teem with marine life and tropical seabirds.

Visit from August to September for calm, clear waters ideal for swimming, snorkelling and diving, or from November to April for surfing. Powerful waves break off the rock formations onto neighbouring Cacimba do Padre beach when the swell rolls in; it's on this headland you'll find the short trail that leads to Baía dos Porcos, most safely attempted at low tide.

GETTING THERE
Located 326 miles (525km) from Recife and 217 miles (350km) from Natal, Fernando de Noronha is serviced by direct domestic flights from Recife and Natal, with connections to other Brazilian cities. Baía dos Porcos sits roughly at the centre of the island's north coast; there is a local bus and taxis, but renting a buggy is the most convenient way to get around the relatively small island.

Gardner Bay

ISLA ESPAÑOLA, GALAPAGOS ISLANDS

ECUADOR

RISING FROM THE DEPTHS of the Pacific Ocean some five million years ago, the isolated Galapagos Islands have taken on almost-mythological status as a showcase of biodiversity – one of the few places on Earth where a cornucopia of creatures found nowhere else act as if humans are nothing more than slightly pesky paparazzi.

Each island in this remote volcanic archipelago, 600 miles (1000km) west of mainland Ecuador, reveals a unique set of highlights. On uninhabited Isla Española, the southernmost island in the Galapagos, glorious Gardner Bay is among them. A key stop on multi-day adventure cruise itineraries, the long, wide, sugar-white beach lapped by turquoise water provides a spectacular backdrop for photographing the colony of sea lions that loves to loll about on its sands, from a respectful distance of course.

A stroll along the beach is likely to reveal plenty more wildlife, from prehistoric-looking marine iguanas to blue-footed boobies, scarlet-hued Sally Lightfoot crabs scuttling around the rocks and maybe an endemic lava lizard or two basking on the foreshore. Don't forget to look up for the waved albatross – Española is the only place on the planet where these spellbinding seabirds nest. You might even be lucky enough to spot an Española giant tortoise. Numbering just 14 individuals in the 1960s, the species has since been brought back from the brink by conservationists thanks in part to a successful breeding program, with approximately 2000 young tortoises on Española now thought to be thriving.

A swim at Gardner Bay is obligatory if time and sea conditions permit – a curious sea lion or two may even join you. Snorkelling is also recommended, especially around the small semi-submerged tuff cone located in front of the beach, where whitetip reef sharks, turtles, rays, sea lions and a variety of colourful fish can be spotted.

GETTING THERE
The only way to reach Isla Española, other than by multi-day cruise, is via a tour from nearby Isla San Cristóbal, which can be reached by boat from the main island of Santa Cruz, or by plane from Guayaquil or Quito on mainland Ecuador.

Playa Manuel Antonio

**PARQUE NACIONAL
MANUEL ANTONIO**
COSTA RICA

COSTA RICA'S SMALLEST national park packs an almighty punch, teeming with wildlife and blessed with some of the nation's most scenic stretches of sand. Punta Catedral (Cathedral Point), with its forest-topped cliffs, was once an island but is now connected to the coast by a thin peninsula. This land bridge now forms the spine separating the park's two most popular beaches, Playa Espadilla Sur and Playa Manuel Antonio. The smaller of the two beaches, Playa Manuel Antonio is arguably the finest, with blonde sand and calm turquoise water beckoning

visitors to take a refreshing dip after exploring the park's 10 walking trails. Challenge yourself to spot all three species of monkey (howler, white-faced and squirrel) found in the park, as well as sloths, toucans, iguanas and more.

While no outside food is allowed in the national park (bags are checked), you can bring a reusable water bottle, and there's a small restaurant, which also offers drinking water refills. There are bathrooms at the main entrance and at a few other spots around the park, with showers and changing rooms near the beach. With a cap on daily visitors, it's worth booking your entry ticket in advance, especially during the December-to-April peak season. Wildlife-spotting walking tours are also highly recommended.

GETTING THERE
Most local hotels line the road linking Quepos and the park entrance, about a 10-minute drive away. It's about a one-hour drive from Uvita, and three hours from San Jose. The national park closes on Tuesdays.

© Matteo Colombo / Getty Images

Playa Bahía de las Águilas

PEDERNALES
DOMINICAN REPUBLIC

~~~~~~

FIVE MILES (8KM) OF FINE, rose-tinted sand lapped by a shock of turquoise water, Bahía de las Águilas is just as dreamy as it sounds. Surrounded by the subtropical dry forests of Parque Nacional Jaragua, the largest protected area in the Dominican Republic, the beach's untouched feel (read: no facilities) only adds to its appeal.

While it is possible to get to the beach by a rough, sandy road, most visitors take a 15-minute boat ride from Cueva los Pescadores, the next bay around to the north. There are a couple of places to stay and eat here, including a campground, but most travellers base themselves at the border town of Pedernales, another 15.5 miles (25km) further north.

If you're self-driving from Pedernales, look out for the 'Los Pozos de Romeo' sign, about 9.3 miles (15km) south of Pedernales. Not far from the road lies a cluster of gin-clear freshwater pools (*pozo* means 'well' in English) that beckon a refreshing dip.

~~~~~~

GETTING THERE
Pedernales is 186.4 miles (300km) west of the capital Santo Domingo. The journey takes around 5½ hours by bus.

Playa Holbox

ISLA HOLBOX, QUINTANA ROO
MEXICO

CURLING AROUND THE NORTHEASTERN TIP of the Yucatán Peninsula, long, skinny Isla Holbox (hol-bosh) is all sandy streets, colourful Caribbean buildings, sun-drunk dogs, and sand so fine its texture is nearly clay. The greenish waters attain their unique colour from the mixing of ocean currents, and on land there's a mixing too: of locals and tourists, the latter hoping to escape the hubbub of Cancún.

'Hoping' is the operative word, because while there are no throbbing nightclubs here, it's not entirely peaceful, what with the throngs of people and constant buzzing of noisy gasoline-powered

golf carts. Yet the island's long shallow beach is nonetheless lovely, with calm waters stretching to the horizon.

If you can tear yourself away from your sunbed, plentiful wildlife-watching opportunities await. Lying within the Yum Balam Reserve, the island is home to more than 150 bird species, including roseate spoonbills, pelicans, herons, ibis and flamingos. In summer, whale sharks congregate nearby, and Isla Holbox is best place in Mexico to book a snorkelling tour with these gentle giants of the sea.

GETTING THERE
Buses from Cancún to Chiquila take around 3½ hours. From here ferries run to Isla Holbox every 30 minutes from 5am to 8.30pm (15-minute journey time).

Tulum

YUCATÁN PENINSULA, QUINTANA ROO
MEXICO

~~~~~~~

INHABITED AS EARLY as 564 CE, Tulum is one of the most visited archaeological zones in Mexico and for good reason: it's sublime. The ruins sit on spectacular seaside cliffs, high above the Caribbean Sea. The structures themselves are modest in comparison to other grand Maya cities, yet Tulum captures your imagination like no other, conjuring visions of pre-Columbian tradesmen arriving in canoes laden with goods, and the Maya workers who received them, contemplating the same mesmerising views.

Tulum is one of the few Maya ruins with a beach – two, in fact – the ancient structures sitting like sentinels above them. Add to that the limestone cliffs, palm-studded white sands and the tropical cyan waters, and bringing your swimwear is a no-brainer. The main beach (Playa Ruinas) is beneath El Castillo, at the bottom of a steep wood staircase. By late morning, it's often crowded with visitors playing in the waves and posing on the sand. Arguably even lovelier is Playita Tortuga, just below the Templo del Dios de Viento. Reachable by a sandy trail, it's typically cordoned off but it's a popular spot for selfies. Though the view from the cliffs is arguably better.

~~~~~~~

GETTING THERE
Tulum's two beaches are only accessible via the ruins. The visitor complex is just off Hwy 307, on the outskirts of Tulum town. From there, it's under a mile (1.6km) to the ticket booth and archaeological site – a trolley shuttles people or you can just hoof it. You can also catch a taxi or drive, with plenty of parking available. Alternatively Tulum's beach road becomes pedestrian-only, it's about a 131ft (400m) walk to the ticket booth.

Playa Balandra

LA PAZ, BAJA CALIFORNIA SUR
MEXICO

THE MOST BEAUTIFUL IN A SERIES of beaches north of La Paz, Playa Balandra is an enclosed cove with shallow turquoise water perfect for kids. Kayaks and stand-up paddleboards are usually available for rent, and beachgoers can also explore tide pools, hike to neighbouring coves and gaze at the surreal rock formations of Espiritu Santo across the sparkling water.

A protected area surrounded by arid, cacti-covered mountains, the beach forms part of the azure Balandra Bay, with its receding glass-clear waters exposing ribbons of snow-white sand at low tide. With only 450 people currently allowed on the beach per day (with two time slots from 8am-noon and 1-5pm), it never feels too crowded. Avoid the first Sunday of every month, which is exclusively reserved for locals. Chairs and umbrellas are available to rent, but there are no other facilities.

The beach directly to the north is home to the famous mushroom rock formation, a hit on Instagram and the unofficial symbol of La Paz.

GETTING THERE

Make the 30-minute drive north from La Paz in a hire car or catch a bus from the La Paz Malecón bus station, with departures roughly every two hours from 9am.

© Matt Gush / Shutterstock

Playa Norte

ISLA MUJERES, QUINTANA ROO
MEXICO

CALM TURQUOISE WATER? Check. Powder-white sand? Check. Gently swaying palms? Sold! Just 6.2 miles (10km) from Cancún, the main beach on long and skinny Isla Mujeres is a real treat. It still gets busy, of course, but even in peak season (December to February, when booking accommodation in advance is a particularly good idea), the vibe is decidedly more mellow here. Rent a sunbed or simply roll out your towel on the wide beach at the island's northern tip and live your best beach-day life. Margaritas and tacos can be procured just steps from the sand, though you'll find better value eats and drinks closer to the centre of town, just a short walk from the beach.

Feeling restless? There are volleyball nets on the beach, as well as kayaks and stand-up paddleboards for rent. The shallow water is only chest deep, perfect for families and less confident swimmers. Avoid weekends for a more relaxed experience.

GETTING THERE
Ferries from Puerto Juarez, a 10-minute drive from downtown Cancún, leave at least hourly from 5.30am-11pm. The trip takes about 30 minutes.

Máncora Beach

MÁNCORA, PIURA
PERU

IN THE NORTHERN REACHES of Peru's Pacific coast, Máncora is the place to see and be seen by the sea – in summer foreigners flock here to rub sunburned shoulders with the Peruvian jet set. It's not hard to understand why. Peru's best sandy beach stretches for several miles in the sunniest region of the country, while dozens of plush resorts and their budget-conscious brethren offer up rooms just steps from the gentle rolling waves. On shore most of the action is focused on the noisy main street, with plenty of good seafood restaurants and international flavours to sample.

The consistently good surf and bath-warm waters draw a sun-bleached, surfboard-toting bunch, and raucous nightlife keeps visitors busy after the sun dips behind the sea in a surreal palette of warm hues. Year-round sun (and a steady stream of overland travellers trickling through on their way to or from Ecuador) means this is one of the few resort towns on the coast that doesn't turn into a ghost town at less popular times.

GETTING THERE

Nearly 124.3 miles (2000km) north of the capital Lima, Máncora can be reached by catching a flight to Tumbes, followed by a two-hour drive southwest along the coast. Máncora is also serviced by long-distance buses from Lima and beyond.

St Andrews Bay

SOUTH GEORGIA
ANTARCTICA

GLACIERS ROLL DOWN volcanic mountains towards the black sands of St Andrews Bay, which indents the northern coastline of the British Overseas Territory of South Georgia, just south of Mount Skittle. Here king penguins form immense breeding colonies, and due to the seabirds' long breeding cycle, the wide bay is continuously occupied by up to approximately 150,000 breeding pairs. Visit early in the season (October to November) to coo over fluffy brown newborn chicks, and watch in awe as elephant seals fight for dominance. The longer 'summer' days between December and February also offer plenty of wildlife-watching joy as penguin colonies peak and fur seals arrive to laze on the rocky beach.

Whale activity ramps up from mid-February until autumn, while penguin chicks can be seen moulting, as seabirds circle overhead.

The frosty lagoon at the centre of the beach was created by the Cook Glacier, which has retreated over 656ft (200m) in recent decades, while the Heaney Glacier facing the zodiac landing zone has retreated nearly one mile (1.6km). The resulting expansion of the beach and the grassy plain behind it has allowed the penguin colony to grow: in the 1920s, a mere 1100 birds were reportedly counted here.

Needless to say, this is not a beach for swimming – for people, at least.

GETTING THERE

St Andrews Bay can be visited on expedition cruises departing from the Falkland Islands (around 870 miles/1400 km away, or 2½ days sailing), or the South American mainland (typically from Ushuaia in Argentina). For the best chances of visiting St Andrews Bay, which has very tight landing schedules during peak season, choose a South Georgia-centric itinerary.

Cabo San Juan del Guía

PARQUE NACIONAL NATURAL TAYRONA
COLOMBIA

PARQUE NACIONAL NATURAL TAYRONA is a magical slice of Colombia's Caribbean coast, with stunning stretches of golden sandy beach backed by coconut palms and thick rainforest. The park stretches along the coast from the Taganga near Santa Marta to the mouth of the Río Piedras, 22 miles (35km) east and covers some 29,900 acres (12,100 hectares) of land and 7400 acres (3000 hectares) of coral-rich sea.

Among its many highlights is Cabo San Juan del Guía, which feels all the more paradisical after the two-hour hike (or rough 50-minute boat ride) to get to this twin set of turquoise bays enclosed by picturesque rocky outcrops. Despite its remoteness, the beach is extremely popular, so if you're planning to overnight here (in a hammock, tent, or one of the very few cabins rented on a first come, first served basis), you'll want to arrive early, especially in the high season (December and January). There's a restaurant, but you'll need to bring your own water or purifying device. Keep in mind that bringing plastic into the park is banned. The coastal currents can be unpredictable here, so take care when swimming.

GETTING THERE

It takes roughly an hour by bus from the Santa Marta Public Market
to reach the El Zaino park entrance, 23 miles (37km) to the east, with
frequent daily departures. From the park entrance, *collectivos* run to
the beginning of the trail to the beach, reached by a 5.5-mile (9km) hike.
Boats also make the typically very bumpy trip from Taganga daily.

Frenchman's Cove

PORTLAND
JAMAICA

MONTEGO BAY AND NEGRIL might be better known, but the smaller, less developed and more secluded beaches of Jamaica's northeast coast have more charm. This beautiful little cove just east of Drapers boasts a small but perfect white-sand beach, where the water is fed by a gin-clear freshwater river that spits directly into the ocean. Fastened to an overhanging branch, a rope swing was made for selfies.

The area is owned by the boutique Frenchman's Cove resort, which charges non-guests a small fee for access to the tropical jungle-backed beach. There's a snack bar serving jerk chicken and fish, alfresco showers, bathrooms, a secure parking lot and the option of taking boat tours to the nearby Blue Lagoon, a serene coastal lagoon fed by a freshwater spring thought to be some 200ft (61m) deep, and nearby Monkey Island (no longer home to the colony of primates kept here by US explorer Hiram Bingham III in the early 20th century).

GETTING THERE
Frenchman's Cove is 59.7 miles (96km) or a 2½-hour drive northwest from the capital Kingston. Hiring a car is the easiest way to get here, but it's also possible to get here via Jamaica's anarchic minibus network (eventually).

Sugar Beach

SOUFRIÈRE
ST LUCIA

~~~~~~

THE MOST FAMOUS BEACH on St Lucia, gorgeous Sugar Beach (also known as Jalousie Plantation Beach) is spectacularly situated between the island's two iconic volcanic Pitons, ensuring phenomenal views both from the sand and in the water. Like most beaches in the area, it was originally a grey-sand beach – the soft white sands are imported from abroad.

It seems unfair that a beach this lovely is private, meaning you'll need to stump for a room at Viceroy resort, or at least pay for a lounge chair (US$75), to access it. Make the most of the steep chair fee by packing a picnic and making a day of it. Don't forget to bring your snorkel – at the northern end of the beach is a marine reserve at the base of Petite Piton, with excellent snorkelling above a drop-off.

If you have a reservation at the watersports centre, a shuttle will be sent for you. Otherwise it's a long walk from the entrance gate; it feels even longer on the way back up after a day in the Caribbean sun.

GETTING THERE
Sugar Beach is 27.3 miles (44km) or a 90-minute drive south of the capital Castries. A more relaxed way to visit is by boat as part of an island cruise.

Red Frog Beach

ISLA BASTIMENTOS, BOCAS DEL TORO
PANAMA

A JEWEL BOX OF JUNGLE-CLAD ISLANDS scattered off Panama's Caribbean coast, lapped by azure waters partly protected by the nation's oldest marine park, Bocas del Toro is all that's tropical. Panama's principal tourist draw, it's the place to go to feel the sand between your toes, the salt in your hair, and a cool drink in your hand.

A smallish but perfectly gorgeous stretch of sand fringed by leaning palms, Red Frog Beach is named for an amphibian you'll be a lucky beachgoer indeed to spot due to habitat loss, local kids trapping them to impress tourists, and waves of day-trippers during the November-to-April high season. But if you are also hoping to sight a sloth, you may be in luck – these slow-moving mammals are often spotted in the trees lining the pathway from the boat dock to the beach on the island's west coast.

Float or bodysurf in the azure water, depending on the swell, laze in a beach chair, and grab refreshments from the handful of beach bars. Follow the pathway to the small headland at the eastern end of the beach for splendid views across the clear water.

GETTING THERE
From Bocas town on Isla Colón, the archipelago's main accommodation centre, water taxis (15 minutes) head to the public dock next to a small marina on the south side of Isla Bastimentos, from where the beach is an easy 15-minute walk. When you land, you'll need to pay a US$5 national park entrance fee.

Bottom Bay

SAINT PHILIP
BARBADOS

TUCKED AWAY ON THE WILD southeast coast of Barbados, Bottom Bay ticks all the boxes for a quintessential Caribbean beach. There's the translucent turquoise water, smooth white sand, and wind-gnarled palms dotting the shore. But there's also a wildness to Bottom Bay that gives it a certain edge. Semi-enclosed by high coral cliffs, with a set of steps down to the beach, the rarely busy beach feels deliciously remote, despite its proximity to the capital Bridgetown and the increasing number of homes being built on the cliffs overlooking the ocean. While calm days are utterly blissful, the surf and currents here are known to be unpredictable, so take extra care if you're planning on a swim. As you gaze out over the tropical water, keep an eye out for turtles and whales. And don't leave picnics unattended – Barbados' green monkeys are known to frequent the area.

There are no facilities at the beach other than a small shack that rents umbrellas and sun loungers, when attended.

GETTING THERE

If you're not self-driving (you can park on the cliffs above), an island tour is the best way to visit Bottom Beach, 14.3 miles (23km) east of the capital Bridgetown.

Chesterman Beach

TOFINO, VANCOUVER ISLAND, BRITISH COLUMBIA
CANADA

VANCOUVER ISLAND'S WILD, remote coasts famously rank in the top tier of dream-worthy North American beaches, and there's nowhere for feeling the pull of the thundering Pacific quite like Canada's surf capital Tofino. With so many astonishing beaches around it's a tough contest, but surf-tastic Chesterman Beach dazzles for its misty early-morning beauty, fiery west-coast sunsets and astonishingly colourful sea-life hidden beneath the waves.

Just outside Tofino within the traditional territory of the Tla-o-qui-aht First Nation peoples, this untamed beach unravels over almost 1.9 miles (3km), with two side-by-side crescent moons of dusty silver sand framed by cedar trees. At low tide, shimmering rock pools form on the sand, revealing hundreds of colourful starfish, anemones, urchins and other sea creatures. At the same time, a sandbar ripples across to Frank Island, which separates North and South Chesterman from each other – the views from here, of the beach set against a majestic mountain wilderness and temperate rainforest, are a thrill.

With its prime location bordering BC's Pacific Rim National Park Reserve, it's no surprise that kayaking, stand-up paddle-boarding, whale watching, wildlife spotting, outdoor yoga and other activities lure summer beachgoers to Chesterman. But it's still the surfing that wows the most, whether you're a beginner or someone with decades of experience. No matter the time of year, you'll want a wetsuit if you're braving the pummelling waves here – temperatures tend to wander between around 45°F (7°C) in January and 57°F (14°C) in August.

Chesterman is a favourite hub for learning the ropes, with a raft of expert-led surf schools based locally. The calm summer months are perfect for beginners, though September, October and November are considered the top surf months. Winter, meanwhile, brings moody storms that delight photographers and onlookers, along with serious swells best suited to experienced surfers.

Tofino's surf scene first began to blossom in the 1960s, but it wasn't until the 1980s that things really took off. Now plenty of Tofino's 2000 or so year-round residents are regular surfers, while the area pulls in thousands of visiting wave-riders each year (particularly for its hotly contested surfing competitions) and has grown into an important global hub for women's surfing thanks to its inclusive community. These days, many people say Tofino's surf world rivals legendary Australian spots like Byron Bay (see p21).

GETTING THERE

Chesterman Beach is 3.1 miles (5km) south of Tofino, almost at the far west end of Vancouver Island's Pacific Rim Highway; you can easily cycle here from Tofino. Regular ferries run between Vancouver city and Nanaimo (on Vancouver Island) in just under two hours, from where it's a 125-mile (200km) drive west to Tofino – around a three-hour drive or a four-hour bus ride.

Stanhope Beach

PRINCE EDWARD ISLAND NATIONAL PARK, PRINCE EDWARD ISLAND
CANADA

LUMINOUS MARRAM-GRASS DUNES, sandy rust-hued beaches and shimmering wetlands are the calling cards for the wonderfully diverse landscapes of Prince Edward Island National Park, which meanders over 25 miles (40km) along the north coast of Atlantic Canada's pastoral PEI (called Epekwitk by the Indigenous Mi'kmaq people). Quieter than some of its (also lovely) neighbours, Stanhope sprawls for miles and encompasses three consecutive beaches, all framed by rolling dunes that provide an important refuge for the endangered piping plover bird. Boardwalks trickle down to an endless sweep of red-gold sand, where you'll feel nature's pull as you sink your feet in. During the cold winter months, this entire coast gets blanketed in snow, while in summer the water is warm enough for swimming. There's a popular campsite among the trees just back from Stanhope Main beach. Head west along the shoreline past Ross Lane Beach to the red-and-white-painted Covehead Harbour Lighthouse, built among the Stanhope Cape dunes back in 1975.

GETTING THERE
Stanhope Beach is around 12 miles (20km) north of Charlottetown, PEI's provincial capital, which has flights to and from Toronto, Montréal, Ottawa and elsewhere in Canada. You can also reach PEI by road from New Brunswick or by ferry from Nova Scotia. The national park is open year-round, but beach facilities are only available from mid-May to early autumn.

Driftwood Beach

GOLDEN ISLES, GEORGIA
USA

THE GNARLED OAKS littering the golden sands of Jekyll Island off the coast of Georgia are haunting. Even a bit eerie with their spider-like branches draped across the shore. But the trees pull you in for a closer look, whispering of mysteries from centuries past. And maybe even tales of zombies – *The Walking Dead* filmed scenes from its 10th season here. But with kids exploring tide pools and climbing onto sun-bleached tree trunks, the scene is far from morbid. Plus there's a steady stream of brides and grooms smiling for wedding shots among the branches at sunset, making the most of the technicolour backdrop. Once part of a maritime

forest, the trees fell as the beach eroded and their roots were exposed to sun and salt. Some trees may be more than 500 years old while others have collapsed more recently due to storms and the relentless encroachment of the Atlantic.

And no, the island isn't named for Dr. Jekyll. Its namesake is Sir Joseph Jekyll, a friend of colonial leader General James Oglethorpe and a financial backer for the colony of Georgia, which was established in 1733. In subsequent years the island held a cotton plantation and an exclusive hunting club. It became a state park in 1948.

GETTING THERE

Savannah International Airport is 90 miles (145km) north of Jekyll Island via I-95. Jackson International Airport in northern Florida is 65 miles (105km) south. Driftwood Beach is in the northern section of the island. For a wider beach and better access to the trees, visit during low tide.

Grayton Beach

GRAYTON BEACH STATE PARK, FLORIDA
USA

THE SUGAR-WHITE SANDS of Grayton Beach billow like delicate frosting, their ephemeral beauty ever-shifting thanks to winds and waves along the Florida panhandle. They're a striking contrast to the blue-green waters of the Gulf of Mexico, which gently lap the shore. But this one-mile (1.6km) strip of pristine sand, part of Grayton Beach State Park, is more than just a pretty face. The beach's dunes protect three coastal dune lakes, which are a rare natural phenomenon found in only four countries around the world. In the US they exist in just two states: Florida and Oregon. Fed by rainfall and streams, these freshwater lakes occasionally breach the dunes and spill into the gulf through an outfall channel. Salt water then flows into the lake from the gulf, filling it with brackish water and creating a unique ecosystem that attracts a variety of shorebirds.

Divers can explore the modern sculptures displayed less than a mile offshore in the sculpture garden at the Underwater Museum of Art. The permanent but growing collection attracts marine life and, over time, the pieces become a living reef.

A 4.5-mile (7.2km) multiuse trail winds through the woods and along the 100-acre (40-hectare) Western Lake, the largest of the park's coastal dune lakes. Its dazzling blue waters are open for kayaking, canoeing and stand-up paddleboarding.

GETTING THERE
Pensacola International Airport is 74 miles (119km) west of Grayton Beach via US 98. From Tallahassee International Airport in Florida, follow Hwy 20 west then turn south on US 331 and continue to the state park, for a total drive of 125 miles (201km).

South Beach

MIAMI BEACH, FLORIDA
USA

A SPARKLING CONFECTION of sunshine, style and beautiful people, South Beach embodies the good life. One of three neighbourhoods in Miami Beach, a barrier island east of downtown Miami, SoBe dazzles like a kaleidoscope paused. Aquamarine waters lap luxurious white sands while the tidy greenery of Lummus Park unfurls just west. Candy-bright lifeguard towers bring Art Deco whimsy to the beach, doubling as calling cards for the many colourful facades in the Miami Art Deco District. Built in the 1930s, Art Deco hotels along Ocean Drive are showpieces of geometry, colour and function. Caribbean flourishes and soaring palm trees add more aesthetic oomph while neon and nightclubs bring late-night sizzle.

South Beach stretches from South Pointe Park at the southern end of the island north to 23rd St. The busiest stretch is 5th St to 15th St, which also holds the bulk of the historic hotels and Art Deco buildings. From hotels to nightclubs, opulent modern excess is assumed, particularly above 15th. The 7-mile (11km) Beachwalk is an ADA-accessible promenade running the length of Miami Beach. Boutiques and cafes line Lincoln Rd, an outdoor pedestrian mall west of the oceanfront while the Wolfsonian-FIU design museum spotlights the power of art and architecture.

GETTING THERE

The Venetian Causeway and the MacArthur Causeway
are scenic bridges linking downtown Miami with
South Beach. Miami International Airport is 12 miles
west of South Beach. The Miami Beach Airport
Express/150 runs from the airport to South Beach
daily between 6am to 11pm ($2.25 one-way). Buses
also run regularly between downtown Miami and
South Beach.

Venice Beach

LOS ANGELES, CALIFORNIA
USA

~~~

CHEAP SUNGLASSES ARE FOR SALE in every direction on the Venice Beach Boardwalk, a 2-mile (3.2km) strip of Bohemian creativity hugged by weed dispensaries, T-shirt shops and French-fry joints in southern Los Angeles – and that's just the view on the inland side! On the oceanside, palm trees frame the sandy beach and the Pacific, but views are interrupted by weight-lifters pumping iron at Muscle Beach, basketball players shooting hoops on busy courts and skateboarders gliding skyward at the shiny skateboard park – take a seat and watch the action. Jugglers, gymnasts and artists all vie for attention – and a few bucks – along the way. The centre of it all is 18th Ave and Speedway.

Looking north from the beach, the Santa Monica Mountains dominate the horizon. This coastal range stretches 50 miles (80km) west from Los Angeles to Malibu and Point Mugu. The South Bay Bicycle Path is a multiuse trail stretching 22 miles (35km) along the coast. It connects Venice Beach with Santa Monica Beach to the north and Manhattan Beach to the south. Bike rentals are available beside the boardwalk.

~~~

GETTING THERE
It's a 7.5-mile (12km) drive north from Los Angeles International Airport to Venice Beach.

© Iulejt / Shutterstock

El Matador State Beach

MALIBU, CALIFORNIA
USA

A 'POCKET BEACH' IN WESTERN MALIBU, El Matador may be tiny but it packs an oversized visual punch. One of three small beaches comprising Robert H. Meyer Memorial State Beach – the other two are El Pescador and La Piedra – El Matador hugs the base of craggy bluffs overlooking the Pacific Ocean beside Hwy 1. A dirt path drops down the rugged cliffside to a set of stairs that descend to the soft sands of the beach, where the visual feast really begins. A cluster of rocks and sea stacks extend from the cliffs across the cove and into the sea. The largest formations hide arches and caves, which are prime candidates for exploring and photography. Tide pools filled with sea life also demand up-close inspection. As the sun sets, a golden glow illuminates the rocks, casting shadows and revealing treasures not previously seen. On a quiet afternoon the effect borders on the sublime.

With all the rocks, the ocean here isn't great for swimming, but you might see dolphins leaping further out to sea. Bird-watching is also good. For the best exploring, visit at low tide, when more rocks are accessible on the shore.

GETTING THERE
El Matador is 25 miles (40km) west of downtown Santa Monica via Hwy 1, also known as the Pacific Coast Hwy, or PCH for short.

Pfeiffer Beach

BIG SUR, CALIFORNIA
USA

FOR SEVERAL WEEKS IN LATE DECEMBER, the setting sun illuminates Keyhole Arch and a sliver of coastline with a luminous golden light. Whether a message from the gods, a portal to another world or a simple but unparalleled work of nature along the rugged Big Sur coast in California, it's a spectacular site during the weeks surrounding the winter solstice. And spectacular becomes sublime when a wave crashes within the arch, its spray aglow with the ethereal light. After rainstorms, the crescent-shaped beach may turn purple in spots due to the manganese garnet washed down from the coastline's crumbly bluffs. Due to dangerous surf, Pfeiffer Beach isn't recommended for swimming, and it can get windy, but walking, beachcombing and sunsets are superb.

The beach is part of Los Padres National Forest and there is a $15 day-use fee to visit. The road to the beach is rough, narrow and one-way in spots, and prone to closures and traffic backups. Check the national forest website (www.fs.usda.gov) for updates before visiting. Parking is also limited. Pfeiffer Big Sur State Park and Julia Pfeiffer Burn State Park are separate recreation areas along Hwy 1.

GETTING THERE

The beach is 150 miles (241km) south of San Francisco. The turnoff to Pfeiffer Beach is a half mile (0.8km) south of Big Sur Station on Hwy 1, on the oceanside of the road. From the turnoff follow Sycamore Canyon Rd 2.3 miles (3.7km) to the beach. No RVs or trailers.

Cannon Beach

OREGON
USA

HAYSTACK ROCK IS A MOOD. A volcanic remnant formed by 17 million years of uplift and erosion, it rises 235ft (72m) above Cannon Beach. A basalt monolith, it would have been familiar to the Clatsop and Chinook tribes as well as the Lewis and Clark Expedition, which wintered near here in 1805 and 1806. Today Haystack Rock and the beach are popular destinations for beachgoers seeking wildlife and amazing sunset views. Within the Oregon Islands National Wildlife Refuge on the north Oregon coast, Haystack Rock is a haven for tufted puffins, seals and sea lions. At low tide, beachcombers can walk to its base and explore its tide pools, home to sea stars and anemones. Gray whales and humpback whales migrate along the coast in winter and again in spring. Held in June, the Cannon Beach Sandcastle Competition is truly ephemeral – all the entries are washed away by high tide after existing for a mere five hours.

Named for a cannon that washed ashore nearby in the mid-1800s, the city of Cannon Beach is a pleasant place to explore, with galleries, coffeeshops, seafood restaurants and a local history museum. For a panoramic view of Haystack Rock, sea stacks, the shoreline and the dramatic Coast Range, drive 3 miles (4.8km) north to Ecola Point at Ecola State Park.

GETTING THERE
Cannon Beach is 80 miles (129km) northwest of Portland, Oregon, via Hwy 26 and Hwy 101. If you don't have your own vehicle, you can also ride the twice-daily Northwest Pointe bus to Cannon Beach from Portland. One-way fares are $3.50 to $18. Buy tickets through Amtrak or Greyhound. Seattle is 200 miles (322km) northeast of Cannon Beach. From Seattle, follow I-5 south to Hwy 30 then take Hwy 30 west to Hwy 101. Follow the latter south to Cannon Beach.

Sand Harbor

LAKE TAHOE, NEVADA
USA

ON A SPRING DAY, when crowds are light and snow still drapes the Sierra Nevada mountains, Sand Harbor and its lakefront boulders evoke a land that time forgot. Crystal clear blue waters. Ancient white sands. Jefferson pines that soar overhead. There's an ageless and transportive tranquility here – at least until summer when beach umbrellas and stand-up paddleboards disrupt the spell as the crowds roll in. Lake Tahoe, which straddles the California-Nevada state line, is the largest alpine lake in the country and the second deepest. The water is so clear that you can sometimes see objects 70ft (21m) below the surface. You can appreciate that clarity at Sand Harbor, especially if you rent a kayak and paddle its small bay.

Sand Harbor, which is located on the heavily forested Nevada side of the lake, also hosts the Lake Tahoe Shakespeare Festival. On a beachfront stage, this summer-long series of plays and concerts is dramatically framed by mountains, the lake and the majestic pines. For a bit of exercise, you can walk or bike to Sand Harbor on the new East Shore Trail, a multiuse lakeside path that links the park to the town of Incline Village. This 3-mile (4.8km) paved trail is a photogenic introduction to what will one day be a path around the entire 72-mile shoreline of Lake Tahoe.

GETTING THERE

The beach is 210 miles (338km) northeast of San Francisco via I-80. From Reno, Nevada, 40 miles (64km) north of the beach, you'll hop onto the Mount Rose Scenic Byway, which drops dramatically towards the lake on its approach to Incline Village.

Assateague Island National Seashore

MARYLAND & VIRGINIA

USA

WITH WILD HORSES GALLOPING across its wind-swept beaches, Assateague Island National Seashore exudes a surprisingly feral vibe, a rarity along the highly developed shores of the Mid-Atlantic. Thick maritime forests and rugged dunes round out the dramatic scene. A barrier island, Assateague hugs the coast of Maryland and Virginia on the Eastern Shore, a three-hour drive from Washington, DC. With camping permitted on the beach, it's easy for city dwellers to dig into its untamed splendour – and wake up to gorgeous sunrises. The park's 37-mile (59km) beachfront is divided by the Maryland-Virginia state line. Low-key adventuring is a hallmark of the Maryland side, with hiking on nature trails, kayaking in bayside marshes and 4 miles (6.4km) of road cycling on Bayberry Dr. At Maryland's Assateague State Park, which is tucked inside the national seashore, there is a bathhouse and, in summer, lifeguards. Stay at least 40ft (12m) away from the horses – they're more bad-tempered than polite.

The Chincoteague National Wildlife Refuge manages the Virginia side of the national seashore, which is an important resting spot for migratory birds. There's a beach here and ranger-led programmes in summer, but this is a place for relaxing and calmly admiring the natural world. The famous and controversial pony round-up – with a swim from Assateague to Chincoteague Island – is in July.

GETTING THERE
The Maryland entrance to Assateague Island is 150 miles (241km) southeast of Washington, DC. To access the Virginia section of the park, you'll drive 170 miles (274km) from DC and enter from Chincoteague. You cannot drive between the Maryland and Virginia sections on the island itself.

Hanalei Bay

KAUA'I, HAWAII
USA

~~~~~

THE LAST PLACE ON EARTH, or a doorstep to the heavens? The difference hardly matters when admiring Kaua'i's Hanalei Bay, a two-mile (3.2km) crescent of golden sand carved from the northern edge of the northernmost island in the Hawaiian archipelago. Just west of Black Pot Beach Park, the photogenic Hanalei Pier juts into the soft blue waters of the bay. Framed by rumpled green mountains and blue skies brushed with clouds, the 300ft-long (91m) pier is the only thing keeping this North Shore masterpiece tethered to reality. The beach is divided into four named sections along the coast. Kayakers and novice surfers flock to the area around the pier, where the surf is typically the calmest, surf lessons are offered just west. Big swells draw experienced surfers to Wai'oli (Pine Trees) Beach Park near the middle of the beach in winter. Swimming conditions vary by location and season but are typically best in summer. Sunbathing and snorkelling are also popular.

Plantation-era buildings in the nearby town of Hanalei hold beachwear shops as well as Hawaiian and health-food restaurants. The legendary Tahiti Nui tiki bar opened its doors in 1963.

~~~~~

GETTING THERE
Hanalei Bay is 30 miles (48km) northwest of Lihu'e and its airport. The Kuhio Hwy (Route 56/560) is the only road into town and it is prone to closures and traffic slowdowns.

Oneloa Beach/ Big Beach

MAUI, HAWAII
USA

THERE'S SOMETHING PLEASINGLY untamed about Oneloa Beach, a broad strip of golden sand in the far southern reaches of Maui. Yes, it's part of Mākena State Park, where lifeguards scan the Pacific from canary-bright lifeguard stands. And most days the Jawz food truck doles out fish tacos and shaved ice to appreciative crowds in the parking lot. But the setting remains feral. A tangle of tropical greenery presses in on the sandy path that leads to

the near mile-long (1.6km) beach – *oneloa* means 'long sand' in Hawaiian – and the Pacific pounds the shore with waves that are an otherworldly shade of blue. Beachgoers should be aware that shorebreaks (steep waves that break near the shore) can be too brutal for swimming.

From atop the lava-rock promontory at Oneloa's south end, views of the beach – which is flanked by the lush slopes of Haleakalā – are magnificent. The mighty volcano erupted 400 to 500 years ago, spewing fiery lava towards the sea. The promontory itself is a cinder cone known as Puʻu Olaʻi, and it divides Big Beach from the smaller Little Beach. Little Beach is a 'secret beach' that was long known for nude sunbathing and a seriously groovy Sunday-night drum circle. Crackdowns on access and nudity have harshed the Little Beach mellow in recent years.

GETTING THERE
Mākena State Park is 9 miles (14.5km) south of Kihei via Mākena Alanui Dr. The park has two large parking lots. The first lot is a mile south of Mākena Golf & Beach Club. Parking is $10.

Ruby Beach

OLYMPIC NATIONAL PARK, WASHINGTON
USA

IT LOOKS LIKE A GIANT emptied his pockets on the shores of Ruby Beach in Olympic National Park. Tree trunks are strewn like matchsticks. Sea stacks cluster like crumbled chocolates. And a colourful assortment of agates, garnets and sea glass add a touch of glitter to the captivating mess. The sea stacks, reachable at low tide, are the public face of coastal erosion here. Once part of the mainland, they formed after a centuries-long onslaught by ocean waves, which also carved out their caves and arches. Flanked by forested sandstone cliffs, Ruby Beach is a wonderland for children, with tide pools hiding anemones, sea urchins, purple starfish and skittering crabs. The shore and its polished rocks – the agates give the beach its ruby colouring – also hold treasures for sharp-eyed rockhounds and seashell hunters.

Two miles (3.2km) south of the mouth of the Hoh River and bordered by a rainforest that stretches east from the coast, Ruby Beach is a wild place – and a fine introduction to the unique riches of the Pacific Northwest. The beach is part of a 65-mile (105km) coastal strip known as the Kalaloch Area, which was added to the national park in 1953.

GETTING THERE

Ruby Beach is on the southwestern coast of the Olympic Peninsula and borders Hwy 101, which loops around the peninsula and the national park. The beach is 172 miles (277km) west of Seattle-Tacoma International Airport.

Playa Tortuga/ Turtle Beach

ISLA CULEBRITA, PUERTO RICO
USA

MOTHER NATURE HAD FUN with greens and blues while creating Playa Tortuga, a crescent-shaped cove on the north coast of Isla Culebrita (Culebrita Island) in Puerto Rico. Here, the translucent waters of the Atlantic change from pale green to turquoise to cobalt as they ripple from the white-sand beach towards the horizon. Deep-green tropical flora blankets the hills that hug the cove, with lime-bright pops of colour adding an impudent touch. The uninhabited island is part of the Culebra National Wildlife Refuge, and the beach is a popular nesting ground for green sea turtles and seabirds. While snorkelling, you may see turtles swimming in the clear water. Large rocks at the head of the cove protect warm-water tide pools, sometimes referred to as the jacuzzi or the baths.

An abandoned 1886 lighthouse, Faro Culebrita, soars skyward from the centre of the island. Shut down by the US Navy in 1975, it is now in ruins and closed to the public, but it remains quite photogenic. There are no facilities on the island, so pack food, water and beach gear. Culebrita is a satellite of Culebra Island, which is 20 miles (32km) east of mainland Puerto Rico.

GETTING THERE
Thirty-minute flights from San Juan on the Puerto Rican mainland leave several times daily for Culebra. You can also reach Culebra via the passenger ferry from Ceiba on the east coast of Puerto Rico. Hire a water taxi in Culebra for the 25-minute trip east to tiny – and hikeable – Culebrita Island.

Trunk Bay

ST JOHN, US VIRGIN ISLANDS
USA

TRUNK BAY IS NO INTROVERT. The marquee beach at Virgin Islands National Park, Trunk Bay struts its stuff like an A-list celebrity, demanding $5 from every snorkeller, sun-worshipper and cruise ship escapee hoping to gaze upon its beauty. But the fee is worth it. Trunk Bay, like hundreds of pretty Caribbean bays, shelters turquoise waters and a quarter-mile (0.4km) crescent of white sand. But the lush, mountainous terrain that squeezes in on the cove adds a cinematic dash of drama. A rocky cay rising from the waters provides an ornamental touch. But the appeal is not just in the aesthetics. Adventurers can don a mask and fins to

explore the bay's 676ft (206m) Underwater Snorkel Trail, which follows a coral reef along the western bank of the cay. Beach amenities include a food-and-drink franchisee, snorkel rentals, beach ramps and an accessible path. Lifeguards are also on duty.

The national park covers two-thirds of the island of St John, which is one of the three main islands – along with St Thomas and St Croix – comprising the US Virgin Islands. November through April is the busy season at the national park. Bring repellant to ward off mosquitos.

GETTING THERE

After flying into St Thomas, you will need to take a ferry from Red Hook on the east side of the island to Cruz Bay on St John. Trunk Bay is about four miles (6.4km) from the Cruz Bay ferry dock. Car and passenger ferries run regularly between Red Hook and Cruz Bay. You can rent a car on St Thomas or in Cruz Bay.

Top 5 Best Beaches...

BEST FAMILY-FRIENDLY BEACHES

Playa Balandra, Mexico

Playa Norte, Mexico

Elafonisi, Greece

Punta Paloma, Spain

The Pass, Australia

BEST BEACHES TO SNORKEL

Trunk Bay, USA

Ta'ahiamanu Beach, French Polynesia

Radhanagar, India

Pink Beach, Indonesia

Sugar Beach, St Lucia

BEST BEACHES TO WATCH THE SUNSET

Maremegmeg Beach, Philippines

Punta Rata Beach, Croatia

Pfeiffer Beach, USA

Playa de Famara, Spain

Cable Beach/Walmanyjun, Australia

BEST BEACHES TO SEE WILDLIFE

Lucky Bay Kepa Kurl, Australia

Playa Tortuga/Turtle Beach, Puerto Rico

St Andrews Bay Beach, South Georgia

Playa Manuel Antonio, Costa Rica

Assateague Island National Seashore, USA

MOST REMOTE BEACHES

Radhanagar, India

Rauðasandur, Iceland

West Beach, Scotland

Haukland Beach, Norway

Gardner Bay, Ecuador

MOST UNEXPECTED BEST BEACHES

Qalansiyah Beach, Yemen

Keem Bay Beach, Ireland

Dueodde, Denmark

Fuwairit Beach, Qatar

Lalomanu Beach, Samoa

BEACHES WORTH THE CROWDS

Bondi Beach, Australia
Ipanema Beach, Brazil
Ao Maya, Thailand
Tulum, Mexico
Sarakiniko, Greece

BEST BEACHES TO SEE NATURE

Tangalooma Beach, Australia
Secret Beach, Thailand
Chesterman Beach, Canada
Cabo San Juan del Guía, Colombia
Anse Source d'Argent, Seychelles

BEST BEACHES TO PEOPLE WATCH

Bondi Beach, Australia
Ipanema Beach, Brazil
South Beach, USA
Platja Illetes, Spain
Venice Beach, USA

LEFT   Pink Beach, Indonesia
BOTTOM   Venice Beach, USA
RIGHT   Le Morne Beach, Mauritius
BOTTOM   Assateague Island
National Seashore, USA

Best Beaches
February 2024
Published by Lonely Planet Global Limited
CRN 554153
www.lonelyplanet.com
10 9 8 7 6 5 4 3 2 1

Printed in Malaysia
ISBN 978 18375 195 5
© Lonely Planet 2024
© photographers as indicated 2024

General Manager, Publishing Piers Pickard
Publisher Becca Hunt
Designer Emily Dubin
Picture Research Heike Bohnstengel
Editors Joanna Cooke, Susie Chinisci
Print Production Nigel Longuet

Although the authors and Lonely Planet have taken all reasonable care in preparing this book, we make no warranty about the accuracy or completeness of its content and, to the maximum extent permitted, disclaim all liability from its use.

STAY IN TOUCH lonelyplanet.com/contact

Lonely Planet Global Limited
Digital Depot, Roe Lane (off Thomas St),
Digital Hub, Dublin 8,
D08 TCV4
Ireland

Cover photo © Antasari azhar / Shutterstock
Authors Amy Balfour, Isabella Noble, Sarah Reid

Paper in this book is certified against the Forest Stewardship Council™ standards. FSC™ promotes environmentally responsible, socially beneficial and economically viable management of the world's forests.